Arab Design

Edited by
Rana Beiruti

Design Doha 2024

Table of Contents

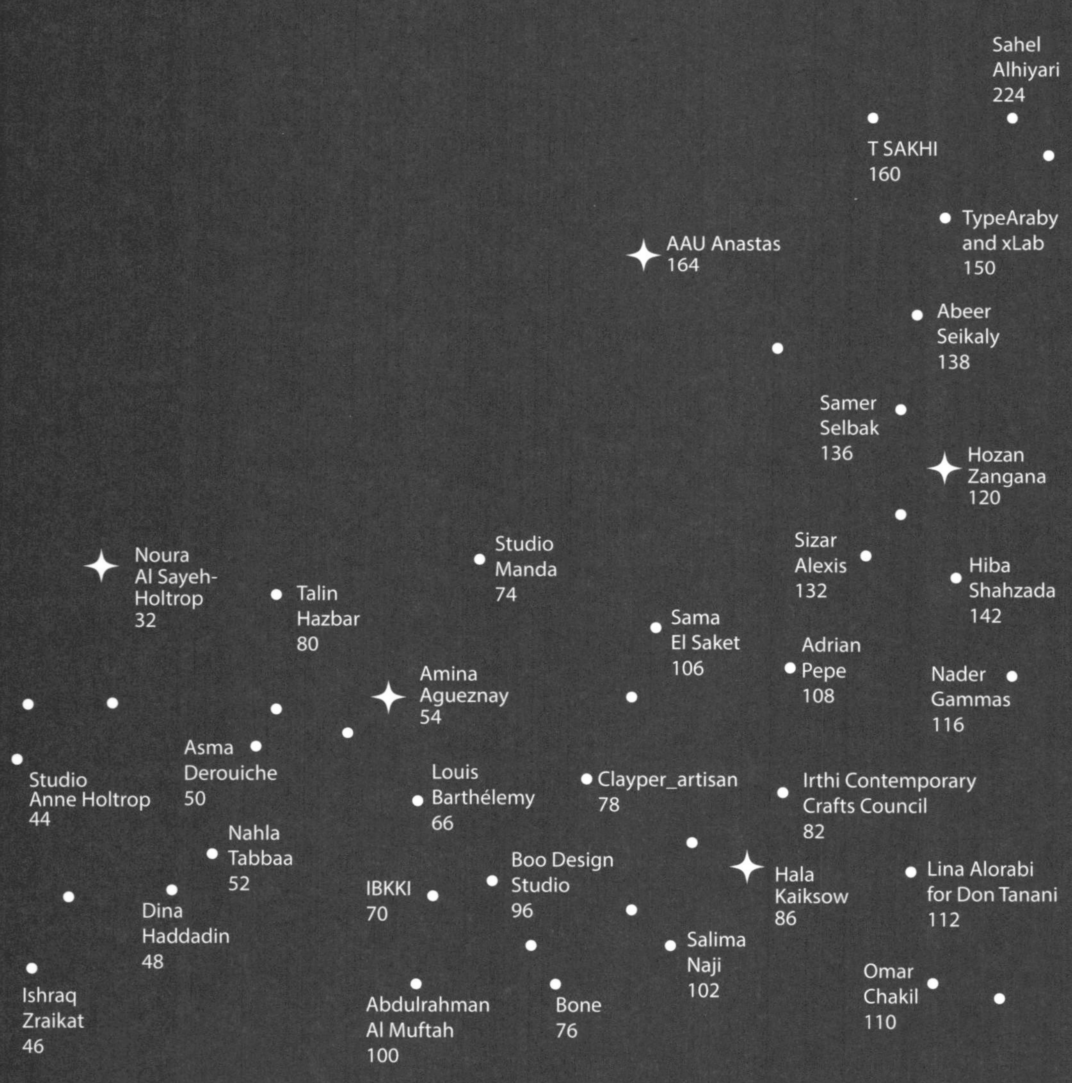

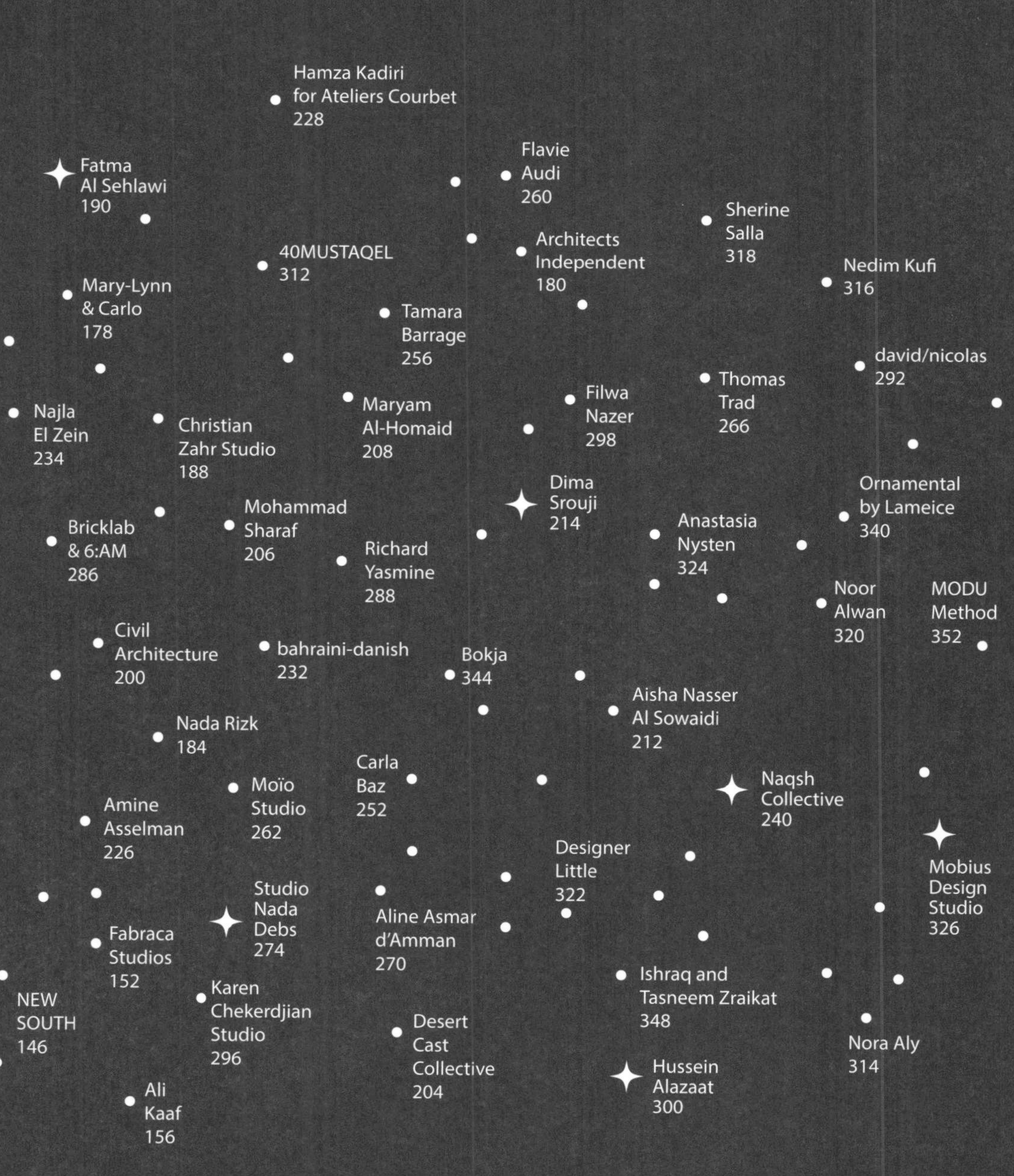
Hamza Kadiri for Ateliers Courbet 228
Fatma Al Sehlawi 190
Flavie Audi 260
Sherine Salla 318
40MUSTAQEL 312
Architects Independent 180
Nedim Kufi 316
Mary-Lynn & Carlo 178
Tamara Barrage 256
david/nicolas 292
Thomas Trad 266
Filwa Nazer 298
Maryam Al-Homaid 208
Najla El Zein 234
Christian Zahr Studio 188
Ornamental by Lameice 340
Dima Srouji 214
Mohammad Sharaf 206
Bricklab & 6:AM 286
Anastasia Nysten 324
Richard Yasmine 288
Noor Alwan 320
MODU Method 352
Civil Architecture 200
bahraini-danish 232
Bokja 344
Aisha Nasser Al Sowaidi 212
Nada Rizk 184
Carla Baz 252
Moïo Studio 262
Naqsh Collective 240
Amine Asselman 226
Mobius Design Studio 326
Designer Little 322
Studio Nada Debs 274
Aline Asmar d'Amman 270
Fabraca Studios 152
Ishraq and Tasneem Zraikat 348
NEW SOUTH 146
Karen Chekerdjian Studio 296
Desert Cast Collective 204
Nora Aly 314
Hussein Alazaat 300
Ali Kaaf 156

Her Excellency Sheikha Al Mayassa bint Hamad bin Khalifa Al Thani

Chairperson, Qatar Museums Board of Trustees

Foreword

One of the most exciting aspects of our work at Qatar Museums is that it brings us face to face with artists who are transforming the way the world looks and changing the textures of the things around us. Every year in Doha I have the pleasure of congratulating the brilliant designers who win the Fashion Trust Arabia Awards. I speak with rising design professionals who are building their careers with a boost from M7, our creative hub, and at Liwan Design Lab and Studios. I meet recent college graduates who are making their move from training to entrepreneurship. And, of course, there are the many conversations with internationally acclaimed leaders in design, who make invaluable contributions to Qatar's museums and other public spaces.

Through these experiences, I know that across the Arab world creativity is flourishing in all the design arts—from textiles, ceramics, and graphics to product design, fashion and architecture.

Awards, exhibitions and festivals have sprung up to honour and encourage Arab design as a vibrant contemporary practice, which has been responding sensitively, beautifully, and imaginatively to people's needs and aspirations today, even as it remains deeply rooted in traditions that go back thousands of years. And yet, despite this surging recognition, and the burgeoning market that supports these artists in their work, no major museum exhibition has ever attempted to survey the entire sweep of contemporary Arab design.

This is the challenge that Qatar Museums has undertaken in organising *Arab Design Now*. This wide-reaching exhibition was conceived to anchor the inaugural edition of Design Doha, Qatar's new biennial, led by Glenn Adamson and Fahad Al Obaidly, and is now lavishly documented in this comprehensive catalogue.

Edited by Rana Beiruti, who curated the exhibition with such astonishing insight and expertise, this book is much more than a record of the show. With profiles of over 70 designers in all disciplines, the book is an invaluable overview of the creativity of the MENA region at this moment in history. Including 'monologues' by 11 of these designers and featuring striking photography, the book is both a feast for the eyes and a rare opportunity to explore in depth the thinking and practice of outstanding talents.

I take pleasure in extending my congratulations to everyone who has contributed to Design Doha, the exhibition, and now the publication of the catalogue *Arab Design Now*.

"Personally, I'm so invested in design because I believe that it serves a purpose in all of our lives. Introducing design thinking to children and adults alike improves the quality of life simply because it allows each and every one of us to live in new ways, innovative ways... Design connects us in all ways that are invisible to the eye and visible to the soul. Design is the backbone of any economy, a sector we fully believe in and support."

HE Sheikha Al Mayassa bint Hamad bin Khalifa Al Thani

Exhibition view, *Arab Design Now*, 2024.

Glenn Adamson

Artistic Director, Design Doha

Introduction

What is design, and what is it for? Those questions have animated a century of invention. It's a well-known story, which begins with the radical formulations of modernism and the emergence of industrial design as a profession in the 1920s. Since then, one generation after another has reshaped the discipline, introducing human-centred ergonomics, the provocations of radical design, the subversive stagecraft of postmodernism, and most recently, an impetus toward sustainability and the regeneration of the earth itself.

All along, though, another pair of crucial questions have gone largely unanswered: where is design, and who is it for? Only recently have we begun to see an adequate response. The conventional centreing of the discipline in Europe and America (with Japan as an honoured exception) has been challenged by bellwether projects like *China Design Now* (V&A, 2008), *New Territories: Laboratories for Design, Craft and Art in Latin America* (Museum of Arts and Design, 2014) and *Making Africa: A Continent of Contemporary Design* (Vitra Design Museum and Guggenheim Bilbao, 2018). Scholars have excavated the previously under-researched design histories of Mexico, Turkey, Vietnam and many other nations. In each case, a new cast of characters has been introduced to design history, while the sense of its truly global, interconnected nature has been deepened.

It's in this context that we have organised *Arab Design Now*. The project builds on many earlier ones focused on the Middle East and North Africa, among them the V&A's Jameel Prize exhibition series, and design festivals held in Bahrain, Dubai, Saudi Arabia and Jordan. (The last of these, Amman Design Week, was founded by the curatorial director of *Arab Design Now*, Rana Beiruti, in 2016.) Yet this is the first major museum exhibition to look at design in the Arab world. What it reveals is astonishing in its breadth and ambition. All across the region, despite pervasive challenges of economic and political instability, designers are drawing deeply on local resources of craft skill, abstract pattern, and spiritual belief, while also responding to the ever-changing currents of the international scene. The exhibition demonstrates without doubt that Arab design is world design, a vibrant context for creativity, fostering a level of collective achievement that is unsurpassed anywhere.

Arab Design Now also serves as the headline exhibition for a still larger project: Design Doha, a new biennial for Qatar. Anchored at M7, in the Msheireb Design District of Doha, the week-long event comprises a range of smaller exhibitions, workshops, a design exchange (for this first edition, with Morocco), and commissioned public works. Our aim is to create a multidisciplinary platform for designers across the region, a foundation on which they can build their own success. Qatar is the ideal setting for such an initiative. A design destination in its own right, with world-class museums, stadiums and public amenities, it is also home to one of the region's most renowned design schools, VCUarts Qatar (established in 1998), and a vibrant architectural program at Qatar University. In addition to a full complement of studio spaces at M7, Doha also boasts incubator spaces at the Fire Station studio complex, and at Liwan, which was beautifully converted from the country's first school for girls under the leadership of designer Aisha Al Sowaidi.

These initiatives have come to fruition under the patronage of Her Excellency, Sheikha Al Mayassa bint Hamad bin Khalifa Al Thani, whose strategic vision for Qatar places art and design right at the heart of cultural and economic development.

What it all adds up to is potential, for Design Doha as an event, for Qatar as a nation, and for the region as a whole. We have seen again and again, in all parts of the world, how the creative industries drive society forward, creating value in all senses of the term and at all scales. Design is no exception – from the job opportunities it provides to individual practitioners, perhaps just out of school, to upwardly mobile businesses, to the dimensions of a neighbourhood, a city, and indeed a whole culture. As *Arab Design Now* abundantly demonstrates, practitioners in this part of the world are already making extraordinary contributions at all these registers, shaping resonant emblems of identity, deep investigations of craft and materiality, and inventive solutions to our most urgent problems. Impressive as all this is, we're still only near the beginning. Not too long ago, design was conceived in extremely narrow geographic terms, drastically limiting its possibilities as a discipline. Belatedly, but rapidly, that narrative is now expanding. One of the most compelling storylines starts here.

Exhibition view, *Arab Design Now*, 2024.

Rana Beiruti

Curator, *Arab Design Now*

Curatorial Essay

Curating an exhibition surveying a region as geographically and culturally diverse as ours undoubtedly comes with a great degree of sensitivity and responsibility. Contrary to the more narrow possible understandings of identity that Design Doha's chosen name for the exhibition may imply, the show does not try to position Arab design as separate from the global condition of design—in other words, it does not try to define what is and is not 'Arab'. Our region's abundant and rich history of design and craft traverses numerous civilizations and is shaped by a fusion of cultures, traditions, languages and beliefs. As a result, it is difficult to separate 'Arab' design from its Persian, Armenian, Kurdish, Amazigh, Coptic or other contributing influences.

Conscious not to flatten this diverse cultural context, I chose to include a multitude of voices and identities hailing from varying places, trajectories, and histories, and to provide a reading of the Arab world in which the idea of collective identity transcends simplistic ethnic or geographic boundaries, and instead relies on alternative approaches to mapping and defining commonalities.

The exhibition therefore also includes works by people who do not identify as Arab at all, but who have nonetheless made this region their home and the base for their practice. Conversely, it also includes Arab designers in the diaspora—those who have been generationally displaced or have sought opportunities elsewhere, and who, as a result, have expanded, stretched, exchanged, merged and blended their design approaches with others, taking them in new directions altogether.

That being said, while the term 'survey' may imply a comprehensive or data-driven approach to collecting and mapping contemporary design from the Arab world, the exhibition should instead be considered a selective snapshot of design as it relates to the pertinent issues that impact our region today. It is built upon a series of dialogues I conducted with designers over several months, and interrogates themes extracted from these encounters that are urgent and worthy of introspection: geography and land politics, architecture and the evolution of our urban spaces, material and visual sensibilities, society and collective culture, heritage and identity, and language.

Underpinning many of the pieces in the show is an iterative and research-based process. For this reason, a selection of these dialogues have been transcribed and included in the publication in the form of monologues, providing important context to the works on display, and revealing the layers and nuances behind them.

The conversation about design in the Arab world invariably begins with the land, and how the unique geographies of the region — from its mountainous areas and deep forests to its large expanses of arid desert — define the material condition and craft histories of the Arab world. The exhibition opens with an installation by Studio Anne Holtrop titled *Sites—New*

Sites, in which large resin casts imprinted by the desert landscape are hung on mobiles, rotating freely, and creating a continuously shifting backdrop. In proximity, the abundance of the region's biodiversity reveals itself, both in a visual and an olfactory sense, via works made from a variety of natural materials, including wool, goat hair, camel leather, palm husk, raffia, agave, and a plethora of plants used to make natural dyes.

Age-old craft traditions and practices are mostly derived from the opportunities and limitations offered by these materials. Today, designers have co-opted and revived these folk crafts, translating them into contemporary forms and applications. Dina Haddadin's *Sabil* borrows from Bedouin weaving techniques to propose a tent-like structure composed of a breathable skin of coarsely woven goat hair. The pavilion, in its complete form, is envisioned to harvest water and provide cooling in the harsh desert climates. Meanwhile, Jordanian textile artist Ishraq Zraikat's piece *Raw Embrace* combines traditional Bedouin weaving with contemporary felting. She works by hand to create a gradation that demonstrates the various stages of her craft, from collecting raw wool from the Jordanian Awassi sheep, to cleaning it, spinning it, and needle felting it, all resulting in a landscaped tapestry fusing wool and goat hair.

Hala Kaiksow's *Charta Domus*, which frames the entrance of the exhibition, is crafted using handmade and home-made paper stretched on canvas and stained with natural dyes extracted from plants grown in her garden in Bahrain. Nahla Tabaa's work similarly advocates for a symbiotic relationship with nature, often relying on seasonal cycles for growing or sourcing materials or on the heat of the sun for processing fibres. In *As Above, So Below*, she co-creates with nature by burying fabric underground to allow the earth's humidity and mineral composition to dictate the subsequent stains on the material. Carefully mapping the passage of time, she then traces the shadows created in the shade of a plum tree, and finally embellishes the fabric with patterns of sunlight using threads dyed with hibiscus, blue pea flower, and safflower.

Contrary to common reductive, often colonial, misconceptions that deserts are barren wastelands with little potential, designers have found them to be a source of great abundance and inspiration, harvesting their unique materials and crafting them using techniques developed over millennia. Focused on documenting disappearing ceramic techniques, Sama El Saket unearths overlooked varieties of local clay available in the diverse Jordanian landscape, revealing an array of possible colours and textures. Similarly, Bone, a UAE-based architecture practice, proposes a modular wall partition using a novel surface material made of date seeds.

This material experimentation and innovation can be seen throughout the exhibition and takes on many forms, often driven by a deep-rooted consciousness about the environment. Georges Mohasseb for Studio Manda combines crushed recycled marble with resin to produce sculptural tables inspired by the desert cactus. Samer Selbak uses luffas, which have been dyed, shaped, flattened and sewn, to fashion lampshades and a space divider. Meanwhile, Talin Hazbar re-purposes salvaged fishing lines and fishing cage ropes, compressing them with recycled rubber grains to propose a solution for rebuilding damaged coastlines.

Underpinning this conversation on the land is a concern with sustainability, in which ancestral knowledge and modes of operation that have proven themselves over time become paramount in a region that is predicted to become one of the most affected by climate change. With this in mind, I carved out space for a conversation about material-driven architecture, and particularly contemporary reinventions using ancestral techniques. One example is AAU Anastas, Bethlehem-based architects who draw on historical knowledge about building through their long-term iterative research project *Stone Matters*, in order to advocate for the return to using structural stone as opposed to cladding. Relying on principles of stereotomy in their installation *Tiamat*, they sculpt a pavilion that resembles a sand dune, while mimicking Gothic-inspired structural systems and pointed arches found across Palestine, Syria and Lebanon.

Similarly, I commissioned Moroccan anthropologist and architect Salima Naji, who has dedicated her practice for the last 21 years to preserving and rehabilitating traditional structures in the deserts of Morocco. Scavenging for materials harvested and produced at Torba Farm in Qatar, Salima and a team of master builders designed and built two raw-earth pavilions in the exhibition space using palm trees for structure and adobe for the 'flesh' of the building. The pavilion features trellises, assembled to filter light and create a protective shield from the sun. The skylights, lined with branch wood, create shade while also enabling natural ventilation.

This unexpected exchange between Morocco and Qatar is evidence of the similarities that exist across geographies and communities. Through Salima's installation, we learn that designing sustainably is not only about material harvesting and techniques, but also about communities. While working by hand has come to define the practice of some designers and builders, craft has rarely been a solo practice. For generations, it has been a tool for self-expression, and a conduit for forming strong social bonds through acts of collective creation. Crafts are never only about a finished product, but also about a process that requires manual dexterity and haptic sensitivity, which can be slow and cumbersome, but also therapeutic and meditative.

Substantiating this is Moroccan textile artist Amina Agueznay, who has built her practice over years in an intimate process of co-creation and knowledge exchange with crafts communities. Working alongside Salima in the village of Tissekmoudine in the Sous Massa region of Morocco, Amina created her series Portals and executed it in collaboration with 24 *ma'almat* (master weavers) in the village. Initially unfamiliar with the materials Amina had selected to work with – namely, shaved palm husk and rough-spun undyed wool – the artisans recreated patterns extracted from motifs found in the architecture of Ksar, the village they once lived in and had abandoned. The work is therefore both innovative in its material manipulation, and preservationist in its subject matter, inviting the artisans to rediscover a bond with their cultural and architectural heritage.

Similarly, Louis Barthélemy's tapestries, depicting lush rural landscapes, palm groves and ancient Egyptian tomb drawings, are also the result of a collaboration with artisans in Mahdia, Tunis. The tapestries employ traditional local techniques in embroidery, weaving and dyeing dating back to the 10th century, and merge materials such as raffia and agave with more contemporary elements such as metallic threads. Exchanges such as this, or like those orchestrated by Irthi Contemporary Crafts Council in the UAE, feature heavily in the exhibition, and are testament to a shared culture that values community, collaboration and co-creation, and is active in ensuring the continuity of artisanal practice. The discourse around the survival of craft communities in our region consequently extends beyond simple preservationist attitudes, or worse, fossilisation and protection. The works in the show suggest that for a craft to survive, it needs to be alive and ever-changing.

Arab design thus flourishes at the threshold where artisanal mastery meets contemporary ideas, design sentiments and applications. From Bilad al Sham to the Gulf to North Africa, designers exhibit a commitment to heritage-based traditions and rituals, and an eagerness to rediscover, reinterpret and evolve them.

For many designers, some of whom are represented by international galleries or have manufacturing partners in the design capitals of Europe, this era of craft revival continues a legacy of trade and exchange of cultures that has always been prevalent in our region. While they may respond to influences from as far as Japan and Europe, their work often remains rooted in a journey of self-discovery, digging into local crafts heritage, and often collaborating with local master artisans.

The Levant, in particular, has always been renowned for its high level of craftsmanship, with great Arab cities such as Jerusalem, Damascus and Beirut historically being important nodes of exchange and trade. Paying tribute to this history are Tessa and Tara Sakhi, whose architectural installation features metal-infused glass bulbs that are reminiscent of marine bodies. Crafted in Murano, the installation references shared knowledge that existed across the Mediterranean, merging the traditions of the Venetian lagoon, an epicentre for glassmaking, and the glassblowing heritage of Lebanon, tracing back to the Phoenicians.

Today, the region continues to produce work with a high quality of artisanal skill and sensitivity to detail and form. Foremost in the canon of regional crafts revival, we find the work of Nada Debs, who infuses Japanese minimalism with Levantine techniques, carrying mother of pearl inlay to new creative horizons. Similarly, Naqsh Collective painstakingly document, record, and reinterpret patterns of Palestinian embroidery, a craft and identity threatened with erasure, while designers in Morocco such as Amine Asselman and Hamza Kadiri enlarge the sphere of possibilities with their local crafts – Zellige and woodwork respectively.

Installations by Bokja and sisters Ishraq and Tasneem Zraikat reference traditional architecture, reinventing the *mashrabiya* (window screens used for privacy) and the *matwa* (an architectural niche used for storing blankets) respectively, recreating and reinterpreting these architectural features using repurposed fabrics. Meanwhile, works by Lebanese designer Karen Chekerdjian, Saudi-based architecture studio Bricklab, and artist Filwa Nazer refer back to the era of modernism in the Arab world, referencing architectural motifs and styles from the 1920s to the 1970s.

In the Gulf countries, the debate between preservation and progress takes on heightened proportions in the built environment, as the effects of rapid urbanisation brought on by the oil and gas boom prompts urgent conversations on the threat of the erasure of heritage-based building practices. This dynamic is discussed in this publication by Noura Alsayeh-Holtrop, the architectural commissioner at the helm of Bahrain's architectural projects, who evaluates the risks, metrics and values to be considered when making bold and transformative plans. This becomes ever-more important in the face of banal, commercially-driven architecture. Her contribution is complemented by an interview with architect and curator Fatma Al Sehlawi, who outlines the vision behind the evolution of Doha and the nation-building and nation-branding process in Qatar.

Documenting this unique moment in Qatar's history are *Bear with Me* by Aisha Al Sowaidi, a gesture of optimism whose title involves intentional wordplay, and Maryam Al-Homaid's woven works *El Bebat* (The Construction Pipes) and *El Hawajez* (The Construction Barriers), which encapsulate the new urban vernacular of construction sites. Taking a more critical point of view, Kuwait-based designers Mohammad Sharaf and the Desert Cast Collective reflect on recent changes to Kuwait City.

It is undeniable that our region has been subjected to irreconcilable ruptures between past and present. All too often, this has been in the form of conflict, war, revolution and displacement. At other times, new technologies, capabilities and discoveries, particularly of oil and natural gas, have transformed the face of our cities. These ruptures, whether detrimental or enabling, create a generational divide, leaving today's designers manoeuvring to reconnect with a fading identity. In this context, 'making' becomes a way of 'connecting' and keeping the stories of the past alive.

Ultimately, what is at stake in the exhibition is this question of Arab identity itself, and pride in the abundance of forms it may take. The quest to connect with lost identities has led to the creation of works that tap into the region's rich and diverse cultural and spiritual heritage, folklore and mythology, with references going back over thousands of years. Ancient Egyptian motifs and narratives can be found in the work of Lina Alorabi for Don Tanani and in the heavy sculptural forms created by Omar Chakil using Egyptian alabaster. In a parallel but entirely distinct fashion, designers Sizar Alexis and Hozan Zangana find inspiration in ancient Mesopotamian and Assyrian mythology, respectively, in an effort to evoke stories from their cultural heritage after being forcibly displaced from Kurdistan-Iraq. Their work carries political undertones, inviting conversation about power and authority. Similarly, in his work *Gilded Fleece,* Beirut-based fibre artist Adrian Pepe invites questions about the value and symbolism of material, in this case Awassi sheep wool.

Undoubtedly, there is a strong element of storytelling in design from the Arab world. Central to this is the Arabic language, a common language that is written using a script so distinctive it has evolved into an art form in its own right. Speaking to this is Hussein Alazaat, a multidisciplinary designer and calligraphy artist, whose installation, *The Beautiful Books Trove*, recreates a project of the same name that archives, preserves and digitises books in the Arabic language. The installation, which evokes an urban book stall typical of those seen on the streets of cities like Beirut, Amman, Cairo or Tunis, features reproductions of children's books, posters and activities, dating back from Hussein's own childhood.

Also advocating for the preservation of our mother tongue and the visual and material culture that celebrates it as an artform is the gathering space summoned by 40MUSTAQEL's rug, which carries the words of Palestinian-American author and scholar Edward Said, questioning why we have adopted the use of colonial languages.

The Arabic letter is the central focus of many practising graphic designers in the region. In their graphic installation, collaborating studios TypeAraby and xLab merge Arabic script and technology to introduce an introspection into the Arabic language, namely the various forms of the word *wojood* (existence). Similarly, Nora Aly's publication series *Beyond the Arabic Alphabet*, dissects and celebrates the semantics and grammatical nuances behind three Arabic letters, reminding us of the cultural values that they embody. The ability to commission new work for the exhibition allowed me to explore a multifaceted view of design and its ability to transform discipline and application. Textiles become architecture in the works by Bokja and Dina Haddadin; a traditional bridal chest becomes a historical document in the hands of Naqsh Collective; furniture becomes an invitation to gather in NEW SOUTH's proposal for a travelling mosque; and a glass column becomes a repository of architectural styles in Bricklab & 6AM's *An Archive for Modern Glass*. We also witness how designers, guided by technology, enter into complex negotiations with materials, transforming their purpose and capabilities. This is apparent in the ways that clayper_artisan challenges paper to become robust and structural, how Hozan Zangana makes wood appear as if it's melting, and how Najla El Zein folds stone and glass into a deep embrace.

From Civil Architecture's 1:1 abstracted scale model of an unrealised architectural proposal to Sahel Alhiyari's evocation of a classical column in terra cotta, these large-scale and ambitious commissions blur the line between architecture, craft and philosophical inquiry. They are technically ambitious but also engaged with both pragmatism and speculation. Likewise, design becomes contemporary art in the lyrical works of Ali Kaaf, which carry important considerations about material and craft as much as they do about the cultural objects they metaphorize.In the field of graphic design, the commissioned publication and installation *Crystal No. 6*, directed and designed by Mobius Design Studio, shows that design can become more than simply a medium for visual expression or communication, but a powerful tool for activating economies and advocacy—in this case, focusing on the ethical recognition and appreciation of crafts practised by South Asian migrant communities in the UAE, and of the artisan communities themselves.

Arab Design Now thus emerges as an ode to the diversity and universality of contemporary Arab identity and the possibilities that design can manifest. The constellation of works presented in the exhibition, and this adjacent publication, capture the multifaceted conversations and preoccupations unfolding concurrently across our region today. Beyond being bound by our shared geographies and unique material condition, what we retain is a common set of values that underpin what can be called 'Arab' design: an intimate relationship with the land, a material and craft sensibility born out of a rich and abundantly diverse history, a culture centred on community, an embrace of new materials and technologies, and a pride in our heritage and language.

"The conversation about design in the Arab World is rooted in the conversation about the land — how the varied geographies of the region produce unique materials, and how people have been harvesting these materials and crafting them over millennia."

Rana Beiruti

Exhibition view, *Arab Design Now*, 2024.

Architect and curator **Noura Al Sayeh-Holtrop**✦ reflects on the shifting conversations on architecture and identity, with particular emphasis on heritage preservation and contemporary architectural practices in Bahrain, as reflected in recent collaborations with Studio Anne Holtrop.

In the Gulf region, where development in the last 20 to 30 years has really accelerated, architecture is increasingly being employed to negotiate and define national identities. Yet the role of architecture in the region is shifting as a growing generation of younger architects are challenging the status quo, rewriting the brief, and moving away from an image-based idea of the discipline.

Architecture is often explained and seen in a didactic manner where it needs to fulfil different agendas; it should be sustainable, produced with local materials, have specific lighting, certain spatial proportions, and so on. For me, though, good architecture is not explained rationally; it simply sparks emotion. It's a transformation of space that makes you notice or feel things differently. It makes you pause.

When I started working at the Bahrain Ministry of Culture in 2009, we were preoccupied with the question of defining a local architecture that is contemporary, but also rooted in what it means to be Bahraini. Our projects were mostly centred around the city of Muharraq, which is one of the better-preserved Islamic cities in the Gulf, distinctive for its historic pearling industry. At the time, Sheikha Mai Bint Mohammed Al-Khalifa launched the 'Pearling Path, Testimony of an Island Economy' project, which had the ambition of inscribing the city of Muharraq as a UNESCO World Heritage Site. The Pearling Path is not a historical path in itself, but rather an imposition of the narrative of pearling and its legacy, both tangible and intangible, on the historic city of Muharraq. The path connects 17 structures that each relate to one part of this narrative: the house of a captain, the house of a pearl diver, the house of a pearl merchant and so on. In addition to the projects that were inscribed on the World Heritage List, we have introduced 17 public squares, a pedestrian bridge that reconnects the city to the coast and four multi-storey parking buildings that help in alleviating the parking and mobility challenges in the Old City.

The Pearling Path project is first and foremost an urban regeneration scheme, which through a very specific cultural and historical lens aims at reviving an important part of Bahrain's cultural identity. The challenge was that there were very few examples that one could compare it to, and to this day we still don't know what the finished project will look like. There wasn't a clear image that

could define or communicate the project in the way that most development projects are communicated. It's important that when we think of identity, it's not treated as a singularity; that we're allowed to revisit, rethink and reassess every few years and re-question the relevance of the work and how it is impacting the city.

Cities are messy and we understood very early on that a masterplan with a defined timeline and a clear mandate wouldn't work. Under the leadership of Sheikha Mai, we were able to work in an organic and incremental way without having to abide by the rigidity of a masterplan with a strong economic agenda. This allowed us space to reflect and readjust as we went along; to learn from what we were doing and to have the opportunity to implement these lessons. There are many things that if we had known at the time, we would have implemented differently, so it's important that we have that generosity to adapt as we move forward. Our aims are constantly changing and evolving, with the opportunity for imagination and reinvention at every step of the way, and with every architect we work with.

Above: Pearling Path Visitors' Centre, Valerio Olgiati, 2018.
Right: Closeup of a coral stone wall at Amarat Abdulrahman Fakhro, 2018.

The conversation about identity in the region also comes with its own complexity, given the diverse communities that now reside in our cities. It raises many questions about who makes decisions, who the city belongs to, and how to create cities for the inclusion of long-term migrants or residents with different backgrounds. When you work in the public sphere, you can't escape from addressing the complexities of society. They become your design brief.

Naturally, there was also an ambition to encourage cultural tourism and to inspire more people to invest in and visit the city. However, given that the project is deeply embedded in the city, it's difficult to really know where the touristic path starts and ends. The most important aspects that needed to be addressed were the requirements of the local community, with their involvement in the process. We had to create solutions that were specific and unique to Muharraq, looking at when and where to conserve, and what solutions needed to be devised for modern living.

Initially, when we would share our ideas with the community for proposed interventions and buildings we wanted to preserve, it was sometimes challenging for the residents to give feedback. A lot of the more conservative preservation projects looked very similar to the existing situation of the city, only a little cleaner and better maintained, which was not directly appealing to them. They wanted solutions to real problems. The challenge then became in defining what kind of new structures we could build next to protected heritage sites, and to find solutions in which these two very contrasting elements could coexist. Once we started implementing the public squares and the pedestrian bridge which reconnected Muharraq to the sea, the community was able to imagine the bigger picture for the city and the importance of what we were doing.

Through the process, I came to understand that there is a very different attitude to building and conservation in Bahrain compared to what you might find in the West. We often approach such urban rehabilitation projects with an academic understanding of conservation and preservation principles. I came to appreciate that buildings here are seen in a more transient manner. In the pearling era, structures were expected to serve their purpose for 20 or so years and would then be

demolished to build something new. If you start looking at the challenges we face in relation to the climate crisis, you can also start to understand that we could learn a lot from these ancestral customs of temporary seasonal buildings, where transience and movement are embraced. In Bahrain and much of the Arabian Peninsula, there were seasonal migrations to different regions in summer and winter; in other cases, at another scale of movement, there were different parts of the house that would be used according to the seasons. Learning about these traditions caused me to question ideas that we have about the conservation of the city, and the desire to freeze certain moments in time. The residents of Muharraq were a lot more open to see things change and evolve .

Left: Interior of the Pearl Museum at Siyadi Majlis, 2022, Studio Anne Holtrop. Below: Interior of Al Alawi House, 2018.

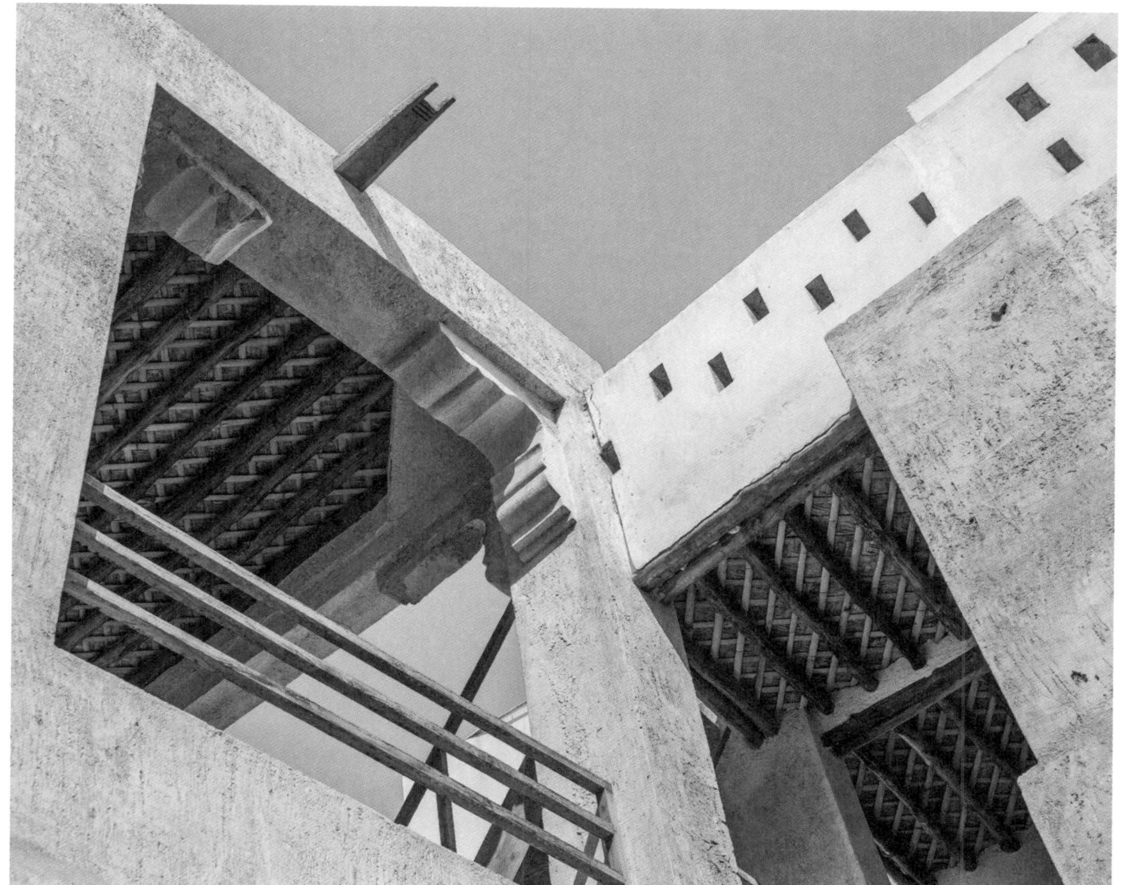

We tend to fall into the trap of very romanticised ideas of the past and idealise the way these cities were inhabited. I remember speaking to an old man who had lived in Muharraq and telling him that we were conserving his house, which as a structure was more suited to the environment and the climate than the ones we build and live in today. His response was to tell me a story of how when he was younger, he would sleep on the roof in the summer, and would have to wake up and flip the mattress in the middle of the night because it was soaking wet. We tend to forget that there was also a lot of hardship associated with these traditional buildings, which is why, when the city started to rapidly modernise, people were happy to leave the historical structures. They were happy to move into a house that was sealed, where they would be in a temperature controlled environment that offered different levels of comfort. We need to be realistic in the way that we look at this heritage today and try not to oversimplify it.

We also often put a lot of pressure on architecture to address issues of climate on its own, in an isolated manner, when in fact the greater part has to do with urban planning and the way our cities are expanding in relation to resources. We should ask where it is actually possible and suitable to live in the summer – knowledge that was more naturally embedded in societies before the advent of cooling technologies, which made it possible to live anywhere. These are much bigger questions that we should be asking ourselves. The projection, specifically for the Gulf region, is that in 15 years it will simply be uninhabitable in the summer. I think that there is a lot of room for innovation in this domain, and the conversation goes far beyond preservation. It requires much bolder changes than the ones that we see implemented today.

Moreover, there is a tendency to put too much responsibility and emphasis on bottom-up approaches, when it should really be a back-and-forth exchange that doesn't negate or erase the role of a professional urban planner or architect, who can assume knowledge about the common good beyond immediate individual desires. The Pearling Path project is a collaborative venture on many levels, firstly with the community, and secondly with the many architects contributing to the work, each with their very specific angle and personal reading of the city:

Exterior of the Green Corner Building, 2020, Studio Anne Holtrop.

GOOD LUCK
SALON

a commitment to preserving Muharraq, while introducing bold gestures and an emotion-driven architecture, commissioning architecture for the benefit of the local community and the upgrade of the urban fabric.

One such commission was awarded to Studio Anne Holtrop, working on the conservation and rehabilitation of several historic properties on the Pearling Path. In the face of challenges related to working with coral stone and the high water table and humidity in Bahrain, it was beneficial that the studio has an office in Muharraq, because there was a learning curve for all of us to understand how and when to conserve. There were a lot of technical issues that needed resolving, and much of the interaction fed back into the process of building. The fact that Anne Holtrop and the team of conservators would work outdoors and build things on-site opened up a whole range of material exploration; the site became his studio in a way.

Bahrain is a small island where logistics can be challenging; so many materials that the studio would normally work with were not available, which obliged the search for alternatives. None of the historic buildings in Muharraq were built with a clear plan, they were often constructed directly by masons and thus have a handmade quality to them. Anne emphasised this by allowing the material to dictate the process. There's an honesty that helps you understand that architecture was made by hand.

Anne didn't have a very conventional architectural education. He first studied engineering, then architecture, then worked for five years with an artist. The studio's work is not channelled by a commission or a client, either; they are constantly engaged in a process of experimentation, discovery, and model-building. In that sense, I think Anne is able to run his architecture practice like an artist's studio, allowing

Noura Al Sayeh-Holtrop

Left: Aluminum casting, Studio Anne Holtrop. Opposite and below: Interior and exterior views of the Green Corner Building, 2020, Studio Anne Holtrop.

his interests and experiments to guide him. To him, architecture that is representational or that resembles existing structures is too nostalgic. He gravitates towards a strong, independent artistic approach that introduces a new understanding of architecture. The challenge was to make it representative of the identity of the place. Through the process of casting concrete, sometimes directly onto the soil, he was creating a record of the landscape, and could produce independent yet locally-rooted forms. Casting reveals the process, whereas drawing is usually representational.

The studio produces architecture that is tactile, physical, and needs to be experienced. There's always also an idea of a space that is inherent to his work, intuitively. He can look at a model he created and immediately have a specific sense of volume and placement. It's not like he creates something with a material and then tries to apply it to a building; the two are inextricably linked. Models and experiments translate into permanent buildings with the same radicality and without forgoing the experimentation. He defines the method of making, rather than the final outcome.

A rendering of an architectural model (1:10) and proposal for Misk Art Institute, Riyadh, Saudi Arabia, Studio Anne Holtrop.

Noura Al Sayeh-Holtrop is an architect and curator, currently working with the Bahrain Authority for Culture and Antiquities where she is responsible for overseeing the planning and implementation of cultural institutions and museums, as well as advising on urban rehabilitation strategies and the creation of public space. Since 2015, she has led the Pearling Path UNESCO World Heritage project, which received the Aga Khan Award for Architecture in the 2019 cycle.

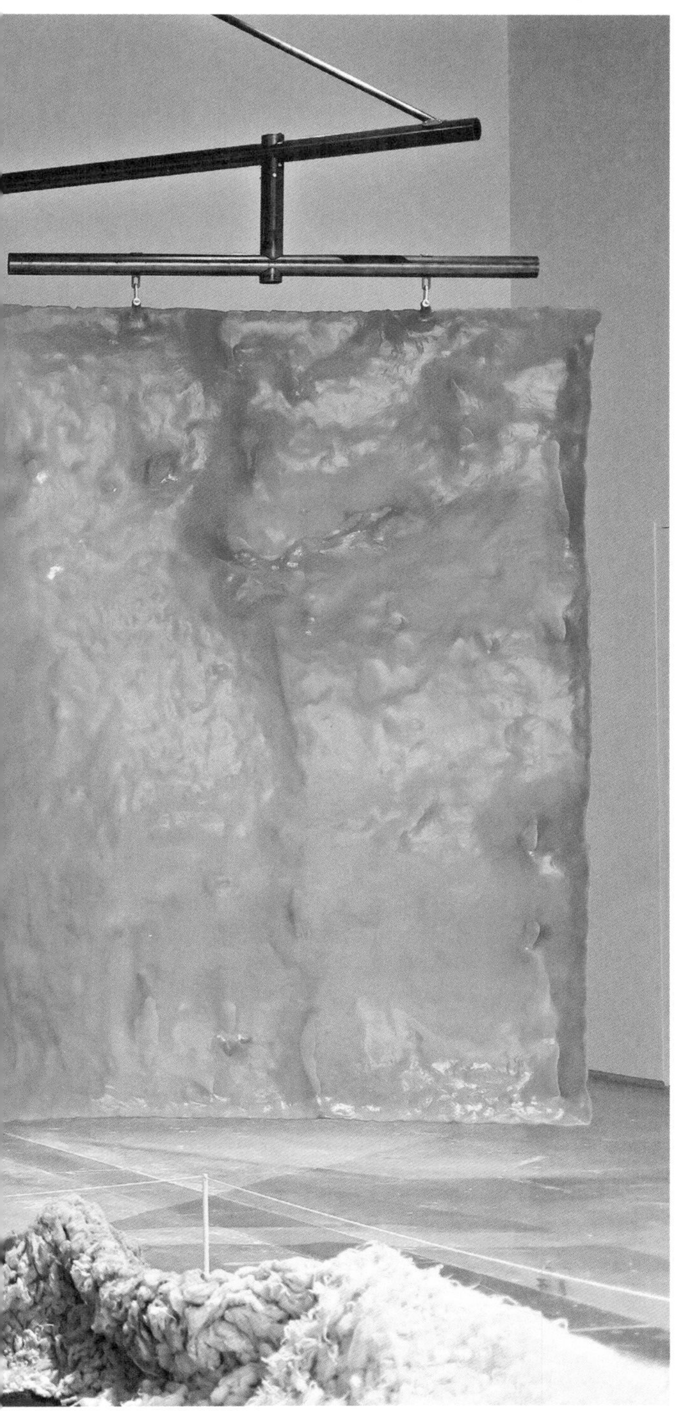

Sites – New Sites, 2024, Studio Anne Holtrop. Exhibition view, *Arab Design Now*, 2024.

Studio Anne Holtrop is an architecture practice based in Muharraq, Bahrain. Continuously engaging in material research and experimenting with casting methods, their work ranges from models and design objects to temporary spaces and buildings. In *Sites – New Sites*, the studio cast resin in man-made and natural landscapes in Qatar. These large-scale 'fragments of earth' are hung on mobiles with bearing mechanisms. As they perform their slowly moving choreography, the pieces alter the spatial configuration of the room and their relationships to each other, endlessly presenting and forming new sites.

Studio Anne Holtrop

Jordanian textile artist, weaver, and wool researcher Ishraq Zraikat created *Raw Embrace* utilising traditional Bedouin hand-weaving techniques as well as contemporary felt-making practices. The artwork embodies her ongoing material research on native Jordanian Awassi sheep wool, demonstrating it in various stages of processing, both manual and industrial. The different colours and textures resulting in the journey from raw shorn wool to clean refined spun yarn, and everything in between, can be seen in the work. The piece advocates for a material return to the landscape and nature's processes.

Ishraq Zraikat

Raw Embrace, 2024, Ishraq Zraikat. Exhibition view, *Arab Design Now*, 2024.

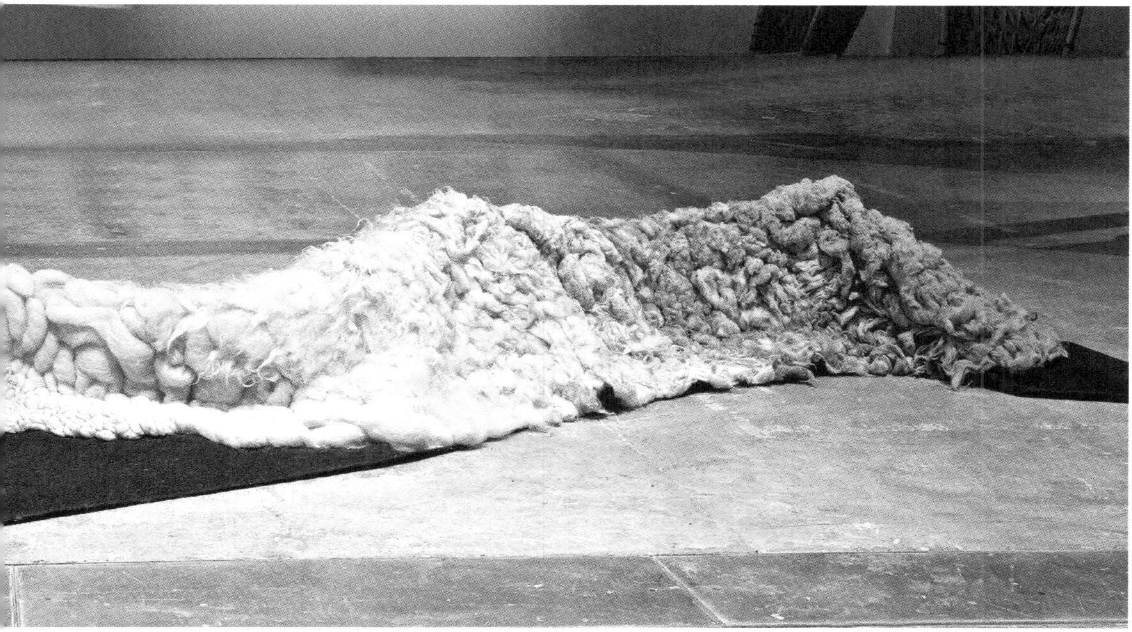

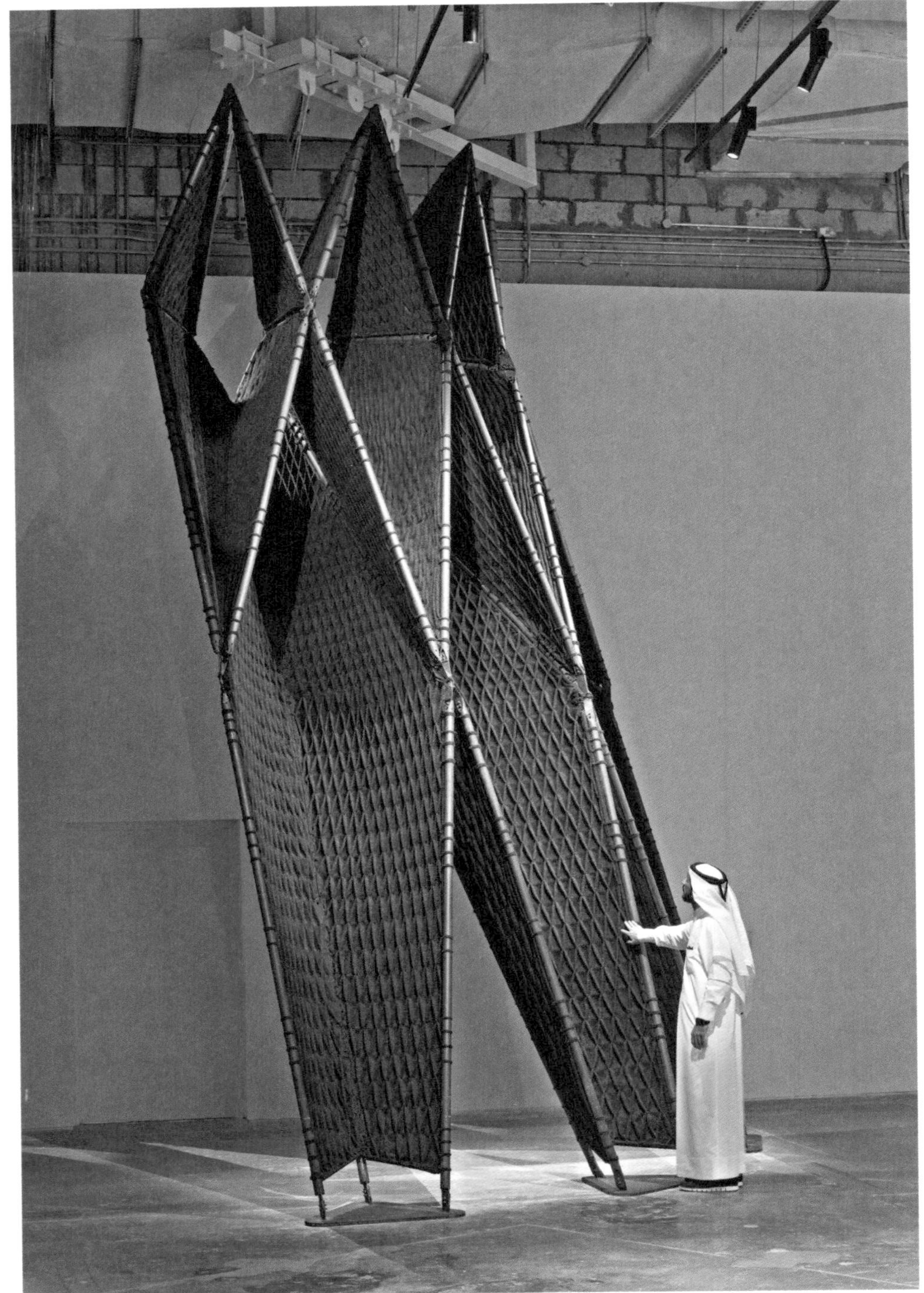

Left: Sabil – *The Nomad Pavilion*, 2024, Dina Haddadin. Exhibition view, *Arab Design Now*, 2024.

Dina Haddadin

In *Sabil – The Nomad Pavilion*, Jordanian architect and visual artist Dina Haddadin presents part of a tent-shaped pavilion composed of nine 'petals' unfolding in a geometry inspired by a traditional 'seed of life' pattern. Made of coarsely woven goat hair similar to native materials used to weave Bedouin tents in Jordan, the breathable skin provides natural insulation. The full pavilion serves both as a shelter from harsh desert climates as well as a water collecting tower, or traditional *sabil*.

Asma Derouiche is a multidisciplinary artist and cofounder of Studio 7 in Doha. She is interested in cultural production in Qatar, primarily focusing on projects that connect artists from different disciplines to create unique pieces. Her work *Wasm* features various graphic motifs and patterns that have been laser-engraved on camel leather. A *wasm*, or tattoo, commonly used in Qatar to brand *halal* (livestock), acts as conclusive evidence of ownership and belonging to a herd. Great importance is placed on the design of these symbols to personalise them, making them difficult to imitate or alter.

Asma Derouiche

Wasm, 2020, Asma Derouiche. Exhibition view, *Arab Design Now*, 2024.

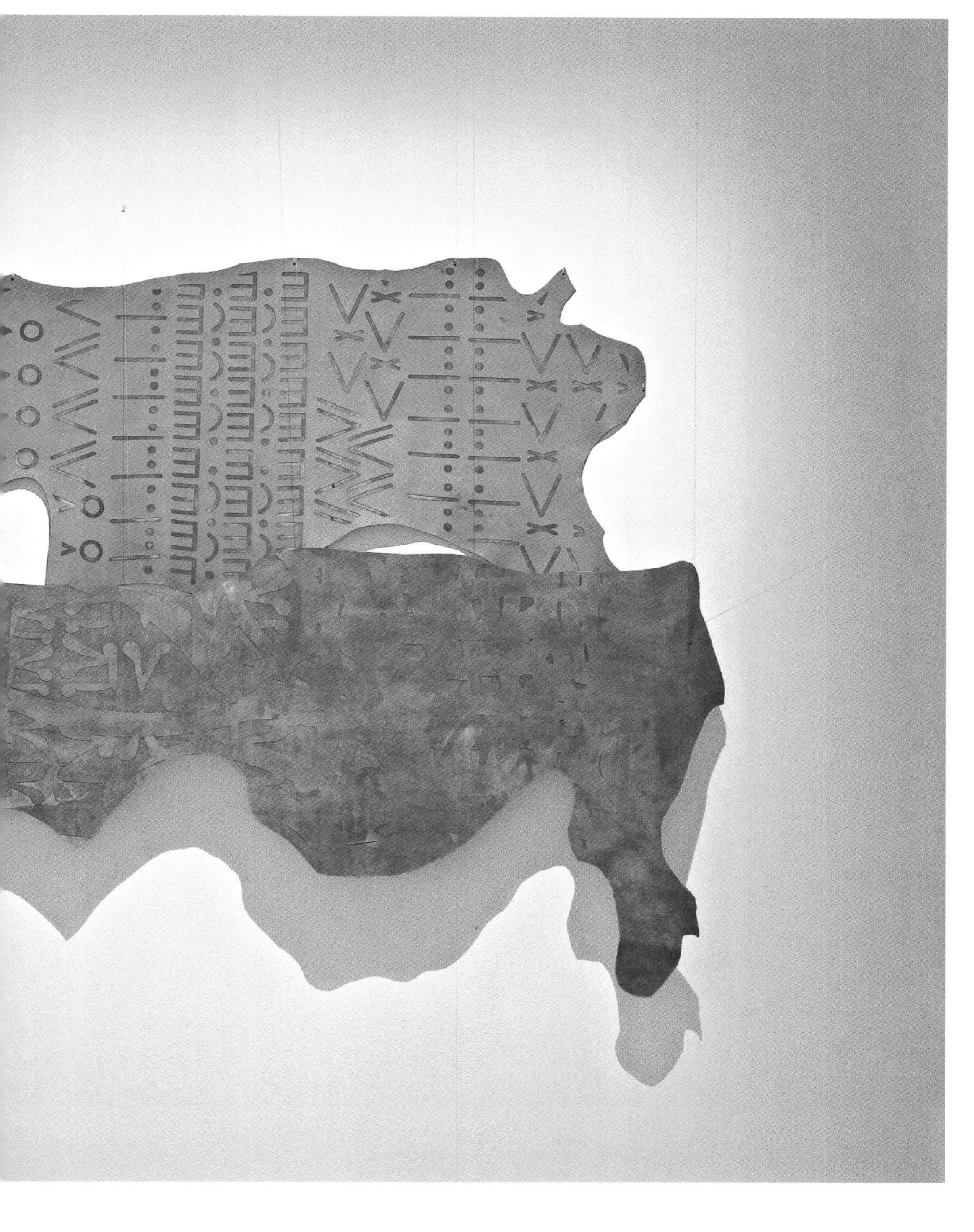

Nahla Tabbaa

As Above, So Below, 2023, Nahla Tabbaa. Exhibition view, *Arab Design Now*, 2024.

Nahla Tabbaa is an Amman-based artist working across disciplines including urban research, culinary arts, ceramics, textile design, and drawing. Her practice is focused on slow-paced, meditative, and laborious methods that experiment with the concept of alchemy in combining organic and inorganic materials. In her textile piece *As Above, So Below*, Nahla attempts to co-create with nature, first burying a sheet of linen under the earth, allowing it to soak up the minerals in the soil, then applying charcoal markings on the cloth to trace the movement of the sun and passage of time. Finally, she applies embroidery using naturally-dyed threads from hibiscus, blue pea flower, and safflower. The resulting piece is a record of the interaction of different elements of the environment over time: mud, sun and trees.

Amina Agueznay reflects on communities in rural Morocco, whose rich history of craft has inspired her to innovate with materials, weaving techniques, and architecture. She also talks about how collaborations, including that with Salima Naji, are a fundamental part of her creative practice.

✦

We have a world of crafts in Morocco, with a different one associated with each city and region: there's the woodwork from Essaouira and Tiznit; basket weaving, silverwork and jewellery making in Laayoune, Tiznit and Essaouira; basket and rug weaving in the whole region of Souss Massa; leather smithing in Fez and Taroudant Marrakech, and so on. There is surely no shortage of craft excellence. The challenge, however, is in the transmission of these practices from master craftsperson to apprentice. This kind of transfer of skills and knowledge is taking place in some regions, with the help of local cooperatives and associations who have become very important vehicles for craft in Morocco. It is with these entities that I found my calling in life: to hold workshops in small villages that keep craftspeople and the ancestral traditions alive.

While I was conducting these workshops, I also learned a lot about collaboration and *tabadul* (exchange). It's through the work with these artisans that I started experimenting with organic materials: palm fronds and fibres, halfah grass (*esparto*), sabra (cactus silk), and then wool. When I started working with wool, I got immersed in it. It's super rich, and I love the fact it's a material that is alive and emits an incredible energy. In Morocco, it's used in rug weaving, or in making the *kharka*, a fine woollen material which has been used to make the *djellaba* (traditional garment) for hundreds of years.

Although I'm not a weaver, when I sit beside the women and observe their work, I can tell what is right and what is wrong. I don't pretend to know the craft, but instead ask them to be patient with me just as I'm being patient with them. I observe what they do, I use their same techniques, and I suggest design changes to the motifs or patterns. A lot of my installations are the results of collaborative projects with cooperatives and solo artisans, and I think of them as a huge craft family that is continuously growing.

There are artisans who like to create and innovate, and some who focus on replicating the ancestral gesture. And they are both valid and important. I don't consider myself an artisan, I consider myself both a student and an *artisan créateur*. In my view, preservation isn't about repeating, but about making the craft come alive with my ideas. At the same time, innovation should not become overwhelming or burdensome for people, with expectations about having to have a specific education or experience. What's more important to me than the product is the artisan. That's where the magic happens.

After leaving my job as an architect in the US, I came home to Morocco to make jewellery. I had no experience, aside from a couple of night courses in New York, but it was important for me to collaborate with an artisan. In fact, I had to collaborate early on because I didn't even know how to solder! My first jewellery collection of necklaces, rings, and bracelets used elements of traditional designs. My mother, who in her youth studied at the School of Fine Arts in Casablanca, used to take me on trips to the South of Morocco, where she introduced me to the souqs (markets). As a teenager, I had a whole collection of jewellery from these souqs.

In New York, finding raw material was very easy, whereas in Morocco, I was forced to be creative with materials early on. I didn't find much inspiration in the city, and much preferred the rural environments that allowed me to imagine pieces of the local landscape in my work. This shift in my context opened up a whole new world to me, and I began to incorporate material I found in the desert, on the mountains, or on the coast. I would work with anything I could find – wood, silk, sand, stones, plastic, fishermen's nets – you name it. When I was invited to participate in a fashion festival in Morocco, I started to really spread my wings. The raw materials became my matter, and the matter was given structure, and it was placed on the body. My work evolved from making jewellery to wearable sculptures and installations. Later, my installations left the body, and became more architectural as I invaded space; the scale started to increase and become monumental.

My journey as an artist wasn't a planned evolution, it was a result of the different opportunities that I had, the people I encountered, and the associations I made that dictated and enabled my practice. Many people are involved in creating a work. Whether it's the curator, the people helping on site, the engineer, or the photographer, there is a *crise prise de conscience* when they become aware that craft takes time. There is value in the slowness of the process in the very fast-paced world we live in.

Meeting Salima Naji was a very transformational experience because she introduced me to the world of Souss Massa in central Morocco. Salima is an

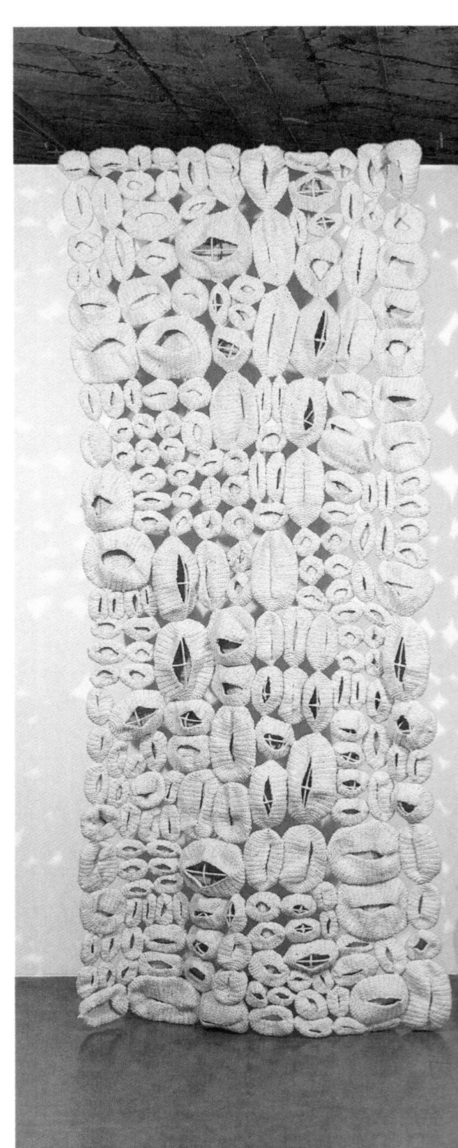

Below: Installation view, *Aouinates*, from *KUBITANA: An Exhibition with Contemporary African Artists*, Vestfossen Kunstlaboratorium, Oslo, 2019. Right: Installation view, *Aouinates*, from the exhibition *Ankabouth*, Société Générale Atrium, Casablanca, 2016.

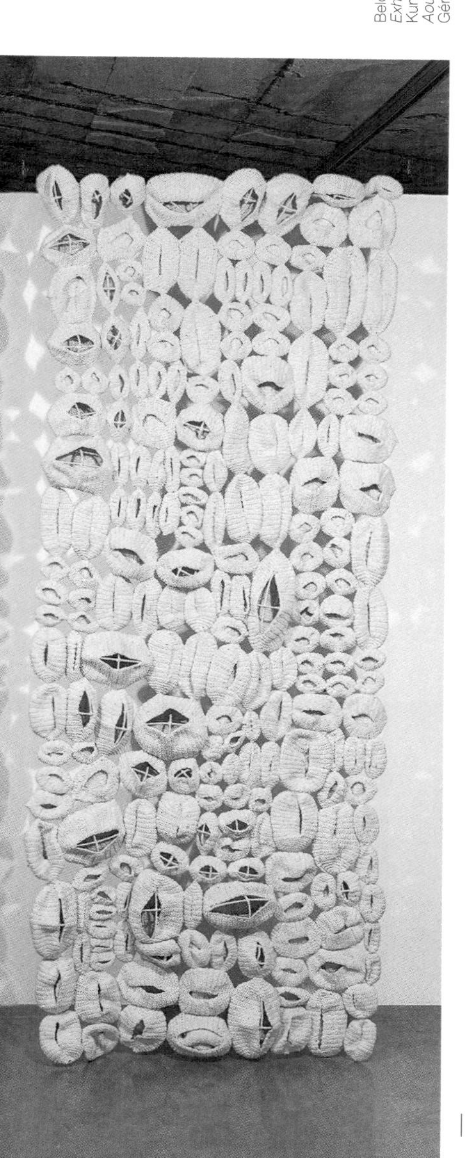

anthropologist and an architect, and she is a passionate person who was born with a mission: to preserve and make people aware of the importance of adobe architecture in Morocco. She is able to read ruins like reading a book. She's a fighter for these traditional forms of architecture, as well as for the empowerment of local communities. She would take me to these sites where she intervened, whether she was renovating an *Igudar* (granary) or building a foyer for the women to work in. I was stunned by her generosity.

The true collaboration started when Salima invited me to animate a workshop with 24 *ma'almat* (master weavers) from Tissekmoudine in the Souss Massa region. She was there working on various site interventions. She would work with the fathers, sons and uncles in the community on the rebuilding efforts, and asked me to work with the mothers, aunts, sisters and daughters on rug weaving, crochet and basket weaving. The workshop was much more about process, ideas and concepts than finished products.

Installation view, *Skin*, from the exhibition *Artistes Marocaines de la Modernité 1960–2016*, Mohamed VI Museum of Modern and Contemporary Art, Rabat, 2016.

In that workshop, I wanted to link architecture with craft, because it was important to me that we create this understanding and connection with what Salima was doing. Many of the women had left the old village where her sites were, so we went on an experiential walk back. There, I asked them to focus on any small details – the doors, the patterns, or any other architectural elements – and to draw them.

I then decided to make rugs out of the motifs of the door as duplicates of the same size. Just as Salima uses adobe and local stone in her eco-restoration, I chose undyed natural wool and *talefdamt* (palm husk) to weave the portals. This selection was important because it's a rough material, and you cannot step on it, which means the rug had to be displayed in a different plane, just like the doors. The women are not used to weaving this material. They usually make baskets out of it and have never woven it into a rug. I found that they were as daring as I was, and they took risks. We did some small prototypes, and they started to understand how to extract shavings from the bark, how to separate the material in water thread by thread, and then how to spin it and weave it. What's incredible is they found a way and organised among themselves.

It's important to make an imprint on people, not just to show crafts in the traditional sense, but also to surprise them. Often when I go to the homes of craftspeople, I find a room that I call a sacred storage. It's normally a stack of rugs or blankets, which they inherited from their ancestors. I always encourage them to duplicate the old ones, or to make a new one based on the old model, and to keep the old ones for themselves.

Crafts are becoming very fashionable and are a big part of the contemporary art world now. The challenge is to begin to perceive craft as art, or engineering, or architecture, or design. I believe that craft combines all of these disciplines. In my practice, there is a lot of building, and a lot is based on modules and structure. In weaving, I am attracted to the form of the line, that when multiplied becomes a plane, and if bent then becomes a volume. These are all basic architectural principles. I like rationality, and my work has to be structured, well-finished, thought out to the last detail.

Amina Agueznay

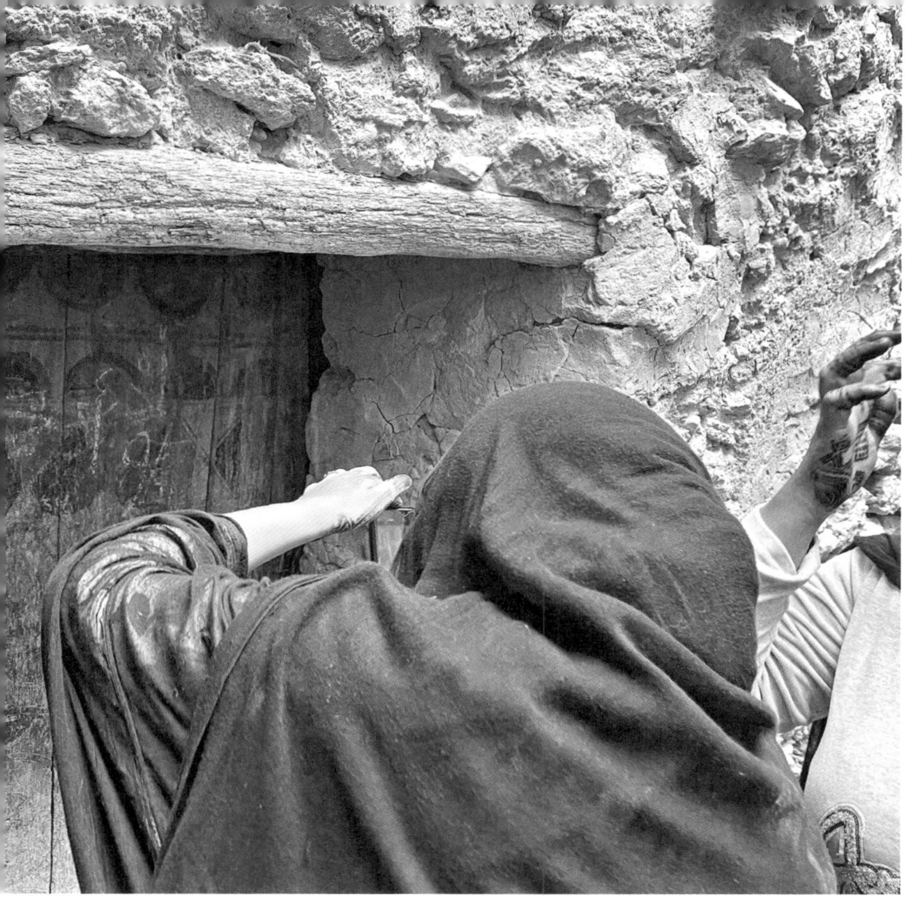

Above: Women Weavers and the Architecture of the Ksar, 2021. Image taken during a design-creative process oriented workshop led by Amina Agueznay with craftswomen in Tissekmoudine (Province of Tata, Morocco) with the collaboration of the Association Gardiens de la Mémoire, supported by the Global Heritage Fund Programs. Right: Behind the loom, weaving Amina Agueznay's *Portals*.

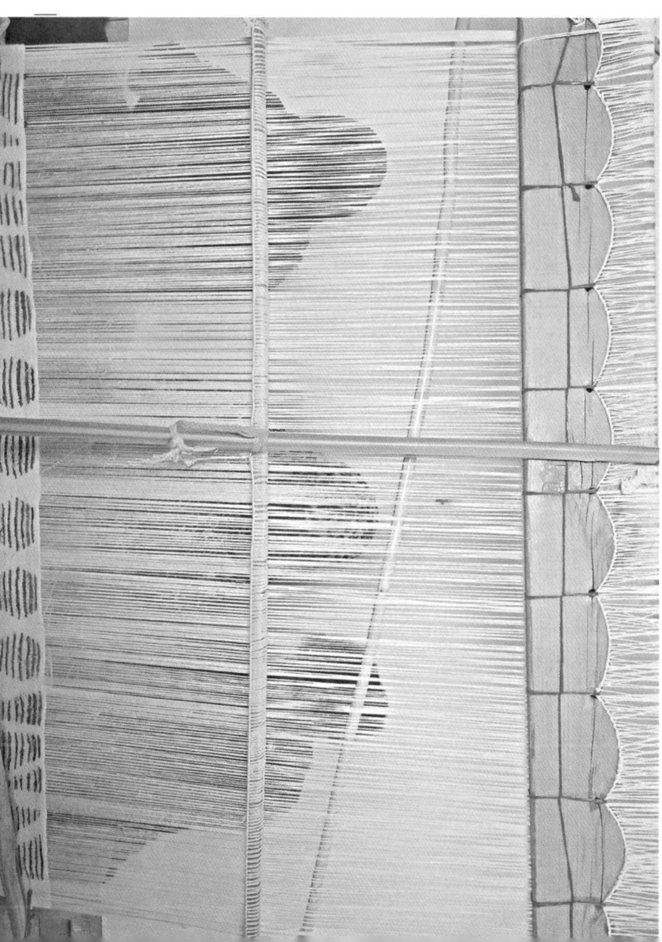

Exhibition view, *Portals* and *Detail Works*, Contemporary African Art Fair 2022 with the Loft Art Gallery, Somerset House, London. Created by Amina Agueznay and executed by Cooperative Tiskmad.

← S01 Loft Art Gallery

Portals and *Detail Works*, 2024, created by Amina Agueznay and executed by Cooperative Tiskmad.

Amina Agueznay is a Marrakech-based artist, designer and architect. Through collaborative exchange with Moroccan artisans, her work centres on craft preservation, exploring the natural world and the transfer of indigenous knowledge and traditional skills. Her work *Portals* engages displaced rural communities in Tissekmoudine, Morocco, with their villages of origin. Using traditional materials such as palm husk and rough-spun undyed wool in innovative ways, Amina invites the craftswomen to recreate architectural elements of the village.

Louis Barthélemy is a multidisciplinary artist and designer, based between Marrakech, Cairo and Paris. His hand-embroidered tapestries, *Manhood*, *Dancer*, and *Gazelles*, depict lush landscapes with stylised figures drawn from ancient motifs. Made in collaboration with siblings Nejib and Zahra and seven other artisans in Mahdia, Tunis, the tapestries incorporate embroidery, weaving, and dyeing techniques that date back to the 10th century, combined with contemporary materials such as raffia, metallic thread, and agave thread.

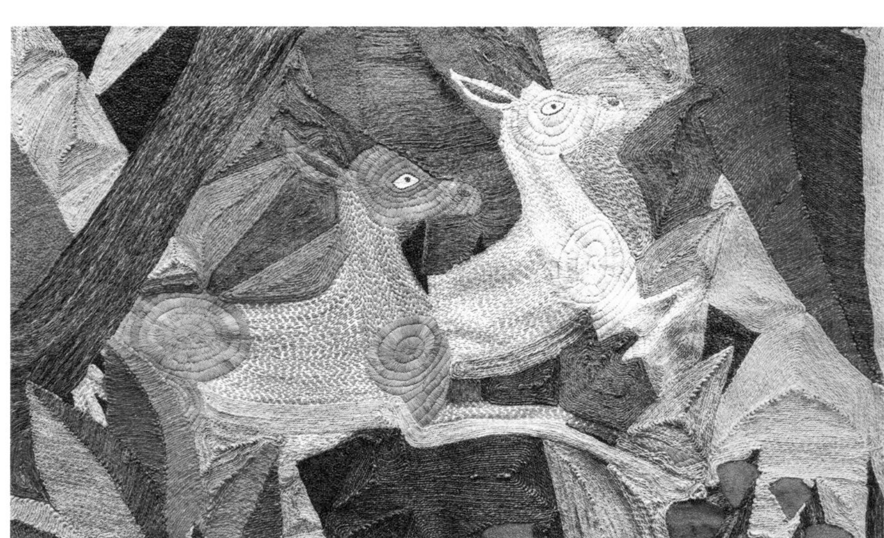

Gazelles, 2023, Louis Barthélemy.
Top right: *Dancer*, 2022, Louis Barthélemy.

Louis Barthélemy

"I am drawn to parts of the world where humans know their lives are hanging by a thread. From this understanding, sprouts the essence of existence: faith in destiny, the power of friendship, an innate sense of kindness, and an unyielding appreciation for beauty. I strive to infuse this profound lesson from Egypt into every facet of my creative endeavours."

Louis Barthélemy

Manhood, 2022, Louis Barthélemy.

IBKKI is a French-Algerian creative studio combining design and craftsmanship, and founded by Azel Aït-Mokhtar and Youri Asantcheeff. Each of their ceramic pieces is created through a geographic exchange, being turned in collaboration with skilled artisans in Kabyllia in Algeria before being brought to France, where they are glazed and fired, often multiple times. The forms and glazes are inspired by the Algerian natural landscape.

The Process Collection II, 2023, IBKKI: Azel Aït-Mokhtar and Youri Asantcheeff.

IBKKI

"Creating between Algeria and France is a way to emancipate ourselves from cultural boundaries and stereotypes. It means fostering our collaboration at the intersection of our heritages with a focus on understanding the different point of view of both parts."

Azel Aït-Mokhtar and Youri Asantcheeff

The Process Collection II, 2023, IBKKI: Azel Aït-Mokhtar and Youri Asantcheeff.

Studio Manda

Studio Manda is a Beirut-based multidisciplinary design studio, creatively led by Georges Mohasseb, and known for its artisanal bespoke furniture pieces and interior design projects made in collaboration with local artisans. The *Cactus* series introduces a material exploration that merges crushed and recycled marble, green resin and terracotta. As the materials bond, they transform into a natural polymer, resulting in an irregular finish reminiscent of the cactus plant.

Cactus Coffee Table and *Cactus Side Table*, 2021, Studio Manda.

Bone

Bone is a UAE-based architecture and interior design practice established by Achraf Mzily and Natalie Mahakian. For this piece, Bone collaborated with metal fabricator Metal Fabrik, and Date Form, a start-up producing solid surface materials from date seeds, a byproduct of the date farming industry. The *Introvert* is an adjustable modular partition, which draws inspiration from concepts of privacy and protection found in traditional Emirati homes and forts, and features minimal apertures fashioned in trapezoidal or conic shapes.

The Introvert, 2024, Bone. Exhibition view, *Arab Design Now*, 2024.

Clayper_artisan is a self-taught artist based in Lebanon. His works are made from paper and cardboard waste and recycled wood. *The Bookcase* and *Les Galets* challenge paper to take on structural properties, and are testament to the creative potential of recycled materials.

Below: *The Bookcase and Les Galets*, 2022, Clayper_artisan. Exhibition view, *Arab Design Now*, 2024. Right: *Recycled Material Samples*, 2022, Clayper_artisan.

Clayper_artisan

Talin Hazbar is a Syrian multi-disciplinary artist and creative based in the UAE. Working across architecture, design and art, she creates responsive structures that showcase the overlapping boundaries in nature, history, ecology, and the formation of society. For her piece *Sediments*, Talin uses 'ghost gear' (fishing lines and fishing cage ropes) that she extracted from the seabed, and recycled rubber grains. The found material is untangled, cleaned, cut, piled, and then compressed to create an installation of stackable tiles. The work acts as a conceptual model for how damaged coastlines in the Gulf could be rebuilt, and how marine ecosystems can be revived to once again serve their important role in the social and cultural development of coastal communities.

Talin Hazbar

Below: 'Ghost gear' extracted from the seabed.
Right: *Sediments*, 2022, Talin Hazbar.

Irthi Contemporary Crafts Council

Sharjah-based Irthi Contemporary Crafts Council aims to protect, preserve and enhance the status of heritage crafts by empowering women economically and socially, through capacity-building initiatives. These include craft exchange programs, documentation, and scientific research for craft development as well as fostering partnerships between Emirati craftswomen and international designers and artists to produce artisanal pieces ranging from jewellery, woven products, furniture and installations. Their collections offer a contemporary take on a variety of Emirati crafts: designer Jennifer Zurick practises *safeefah* weaving on camel leather; Studio Nada Debs merges *talli* braids with traditional Lebanese marquetry; Fatima Al Zaabi sculpts Emirati-inspired elements using handmade clay; Studiopepe experiments with clay and different weaving techniques of macrame and *safeefah*; and Ghaya bin Mesmar incorporates a sustainable approach utilising dyes extracted from natural resources in woven baskets.

Thaya Collection, 2022, Irthi x Creative Dialogue by Ghaya Bin Mesmar.

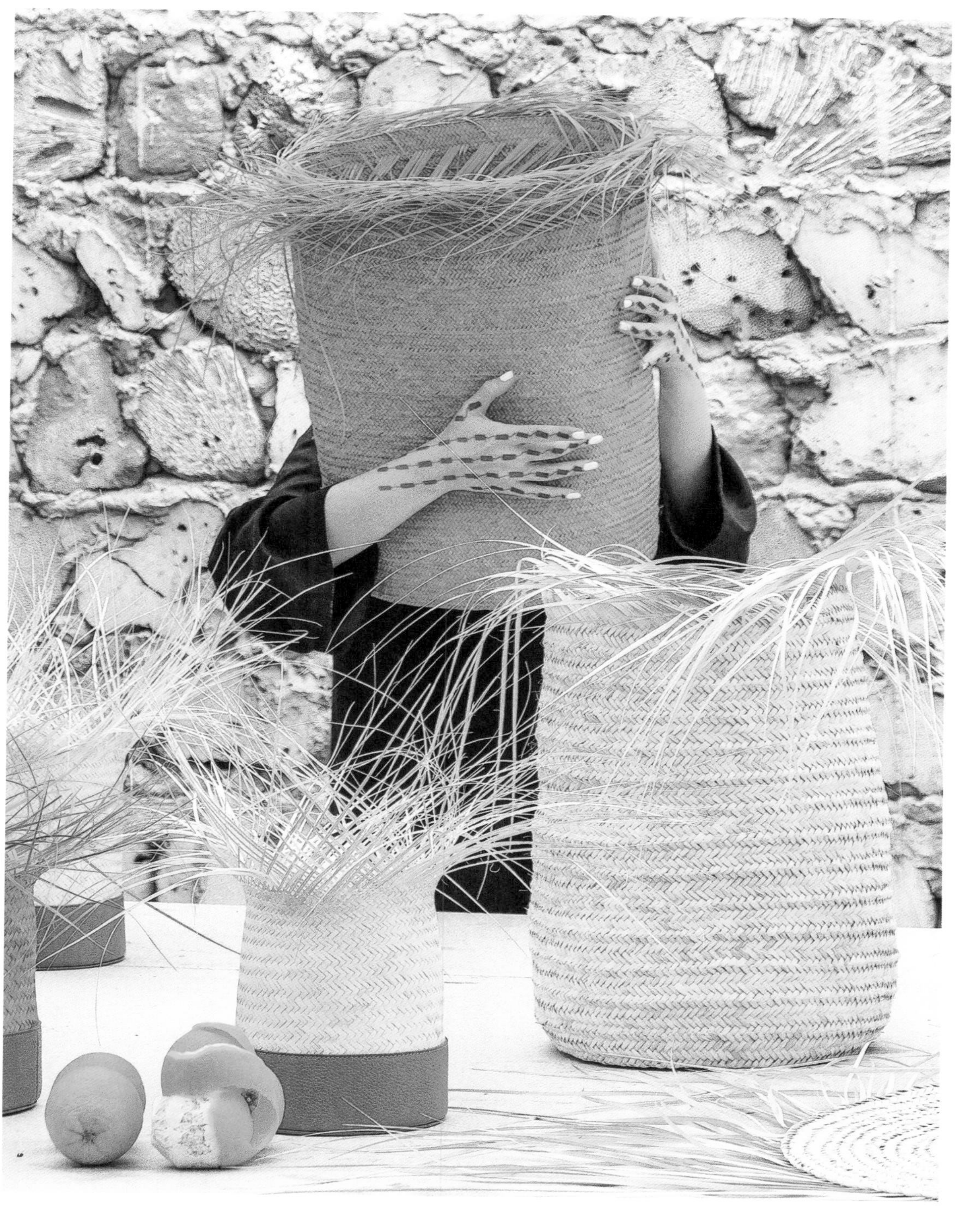

Below: *Sofra Collection*, 2023, Irthi x Studiopepe.
Right: *Nadd Collection*, 2022, Irthi x Fatima Al Zaabi and *Design*.
Below right: *Labs Collection*, 2019, Irthi x Jennifer Zurick.

Artist, designer and sculptor **Hala Kaiksow** talks about creation as an act that starts and ends with the land, opting to produce her own fabrics, natural dyes, and materials – all made by hand.

I've always been drawn to raw textures and materials that recall Bahrain's landscape, whether it's rock formations in the desert, the colour of a traditional plaster wall or the bark of an ancient tree. Being a transient stop on a trade route, Bahrain was a melting pot for the exchange of traditions and crafts, which connected the country with so many other nations and identities and really connected us as a people.

My work is inspired by a myriad of crafts stretching from basket weaving to traditional Bahraini attire, and as far afield as hand felting from Iran, all carrying the commonality of the human hand that is so embedded in the trade. Our collective history is so much richer and more powerful than that of the individual and should be celebrated as such.

Bahrain was once known as the island of a million palm trees; because of its natural springs and untouched land, nature could flourish uninhibited. It has a rich history of weaving with cotton, wool, and palm leaves. These weaving techniques are embedded in our identity as a nation, once used to sustain lives, clothe people, and create shelters; roofs were made from palms, which also added structure to walls. However, industrialisation in the region and around the world has robbed us of the beauty that comes with building using the fruits of the land. While it may be easier to construct a house out of cinderblock and concrete, the woven palm leaves that used to adorn our walls are no longer there to remind us of our reliance on and relationship with nature.

My interest in textiles has been with me since the beginning, when I was studying Fine Arts and creating sculptural works. It deepened during my masters in clothing design, where I started to integrate hand-woven textiles into my collections. Inspired by nomadic women who create their own textiles from scratch, I bought a small loom, watched a few YouTube tutorials, and taught myself to weave. I make my own fabrics to this day in an effort to remain in touch with the land and with craft. For me, the act of making becomes a conversation we have with nature. The technique and materiality of the work created are informed by what nature gives us.

In 2021, I worked with Irthi Contemporary Craft Council on a tapestry piece called *Boma'an*, named after the tree whose leaves we used for the project. I wanted to create a piece that was reminiscent of the *sofras* (floor mats), which people once used to sit on during meals. I love the way woven pieces formed a part of everyday life. Unfortunately, now they feel a little disconnected from our daily practices, and are viewed as souvenir objects that are no longer relevant. I wanted to bring back a nostalgic feeling by creating a space using palm leaves that could invite people to connect both with the tree and with one another.

Today, my practice revolves around celebrating this handwork – from cutting, to sewing, to weaving, to natural dyeing. I embrace all processes that allow me to use my hands. I prefer to make my own fabrics, either alone or in collaboration with weavers in Bahrain or globally. In these collaborations, we share ideas, ideals, and intentions for the work, and embed those conversations into the process of creation. We also make our own buttons and fasteners.

One of my most treasured creations is a felt coat that I sewed entirely by hand for my master's collection. It is made from a raw wool felt and creates a cocoon of sorts that protects its wearer. I think this piece was my first venture into creating shelter for the body and experimenting with taking my sculpture into a tactile medium. When conceptualising a project, I often begin with form and then start thinking about the process of creating it. I consider materials such as raw linen, silk and hemp, and embellish them with fragments of metal, wood, latex and mother of pearl. All the while, I try not to stifle the magic of the process and how it goes on to inform the final work. I try to highlight the process and celebrate the journey and soul of the hand in my projects. I place great importance on age-old craft traditions and in creating garments that have soul, that carry the story of their maker, and protect their wearer – the kind of garments that get handed down across generations.

I want the work I make to defy mass production. In the fast-paced world we live in, handwork has become either obsolete or a complete luxury, and I yearn for a time where it was the norm for what we consumed and wore. As humans in the 21st century, the need for the new and fast has become the standard. Even when you are ahead, you are still one step behind. This has caused an immense strain on handcrafts and creation, stifling originality and celebrating regurgitation. I think there is a need to embrace the here and now, to be in the moment of making instead of trying to be ahead. This

Boma'an, 2021, Hala Kaiksow x Irthi Council: a collaboration between Hala Kaiksow and the *safeefa* weavers of UAE.

Left: *Boma'an*, 2021 (detail), Hala Kaiksow x Irthi Council.
Below: Hala at her loom in the studio, 2019.

begins with addressing the role of the future consumer, teaching them to be mindful, to think about past trends and seasonality, to embrace slowness, and to let the garment live with them for a lifetime.

At the same time, makers also have a duty to preserve modes of creation that are slow, mindful and meditative. I think craft is what is missing from the conversation in fashion today. Traditional methods need to be preserved in their integrity, but also integrated with new forms and ideas. This will allow for the craft to grow and stay relevant, to be able to reach a younger blooming mind that will carry these ideals to the next generation.

This became ever more necessary when I became a mother myself. Entering motherhood changes the entire fibre of being. Your exterior image may appear the same but every cell in your body has rearranged itself and there is a new person you need to now discover. Having a child as a maker is knowing that the greatest thing you will ever create is the human you have given birth to. It is extremely humbling and confusing in so many ways, because you are watching something growing in front of you. It brought together, in a really physical way, my understanding of home, my body as a home, and the act of creation.

This organically seeps into everything I make. I am expanding on this thought and integrating elements of my physical home and land into the idea of creating shelter. The ideas of creating one's own means of protection, be it through shelter or clothing, has become an overarching theme in my work.

Thinking along the lines of integrating my home and life into my work has led me to experiment with a myriad of materials. I like to experiment with natural dyes that can be extracted from bark, flowers, leaves, and the roots of plants, which I have begun trying to grow at home. I love seeing the evolution of a seed turning into leaves and then into pigment that can so beautifully stain cloth. Currently I'm growing madder, indigo and dyer's cosmos, which make red, blue and orangey-yellow dyes. Also, in an effort to source raw materials from my surroundings, I have been playing with making paper from materials in my garden. Paper as a medium has always fascinated me for its fragility, yet rigidity, being both soft and hard at the same time. I think it will be an interesting challenge to create with paper and be able to bring elements of my home into a creative landscape.

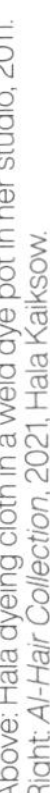

Above: Hala dyeing cloth in a weld dye pot in her studio, 2011.
Right: *Al-Hajr Collection*, 2021, Hala Kaiksow.

Charta Domos, 2024, Hala Kaiksow.
Exhibition view, *Arab Design Now*, 2024.

Hala Kaiskow is a designer and artisanal maker. Her approach to craft is driven by experimentation with the possibilities of sculpting, which extends to self-made hand-woven fabrics and natural dyes. Her piece *Boma'an*, created for Irthi Contemporary Crafts Council in the UAE, is a woven *safeefah* tapestry composed of *khose* (palm) and hand-dyed cotton silk yarn. Her newly commissioned work, *Charta Domus*, is an entrance arch constructed from handcrafted paper and palm and coconut husk, and is dyed using materials sourced from the designer's garden.

Boo Design Studio

Medallion, 2023, Boo Design Studio.

Amanda and Jo Booabbood are a Qatar-based husband-and-wife team with a background in interior architecture and product design. Their *Medallion* lights are inspired by timeless Arab jewellery motifs, gemstones, and precious metals.

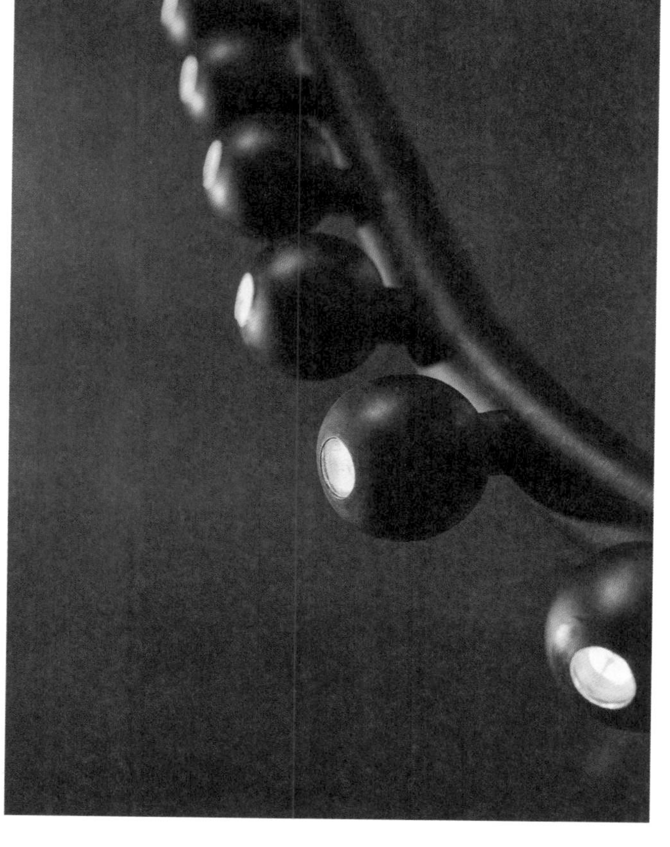

Medallion, 2023, Boo Design Studio.

Abdulrahman Al Muftah is a multidisciplinary Qatari designer whose work is characterised by material innovation and a deep connection to nature and his cultural heritage. *Palm Fibre Carpet* is an homage to traditional *sadu* weaving and draws on the artist's familial connection to professional traditional weavers.

Abdulrahman Al Muftah

Palm Fibre Carpet, 2023, Abdulrahman Al Muftah. Exhibition view, *Arab Design Now*, 2024.

Sharing the Earth (Spatial Interiorities), 2024, Salima Naji. Exhibition view, *Arab Design Now*, 2024.

Salima Naji is a Moroccan architect and anthropologist who has been working for over 20 years in the field of contemporary architecture and the rehabilitation of rural adobe structures in Morocco. For her installation *Sharing the Earth* (*Spatial Interiorities*), she worked alongside three master artisans from Morocco in collaboration with Torba Farm in Qatar to construct two raw-earth and bamboo pavilions that use palm trees for structure. In a style typical of Moroccan rural adobe architecture, also seen across the Sahara, the structure features skylights, lined with patterns of branch wood, to create shade and allow the soft breath of natural ventilation. This installation encourages a complex dialogue with materials, which are the very 'flesh' of the building. By sculpting the earth, her aim is to put the hand and nature back into the heart of the creative process.

Salima Naji

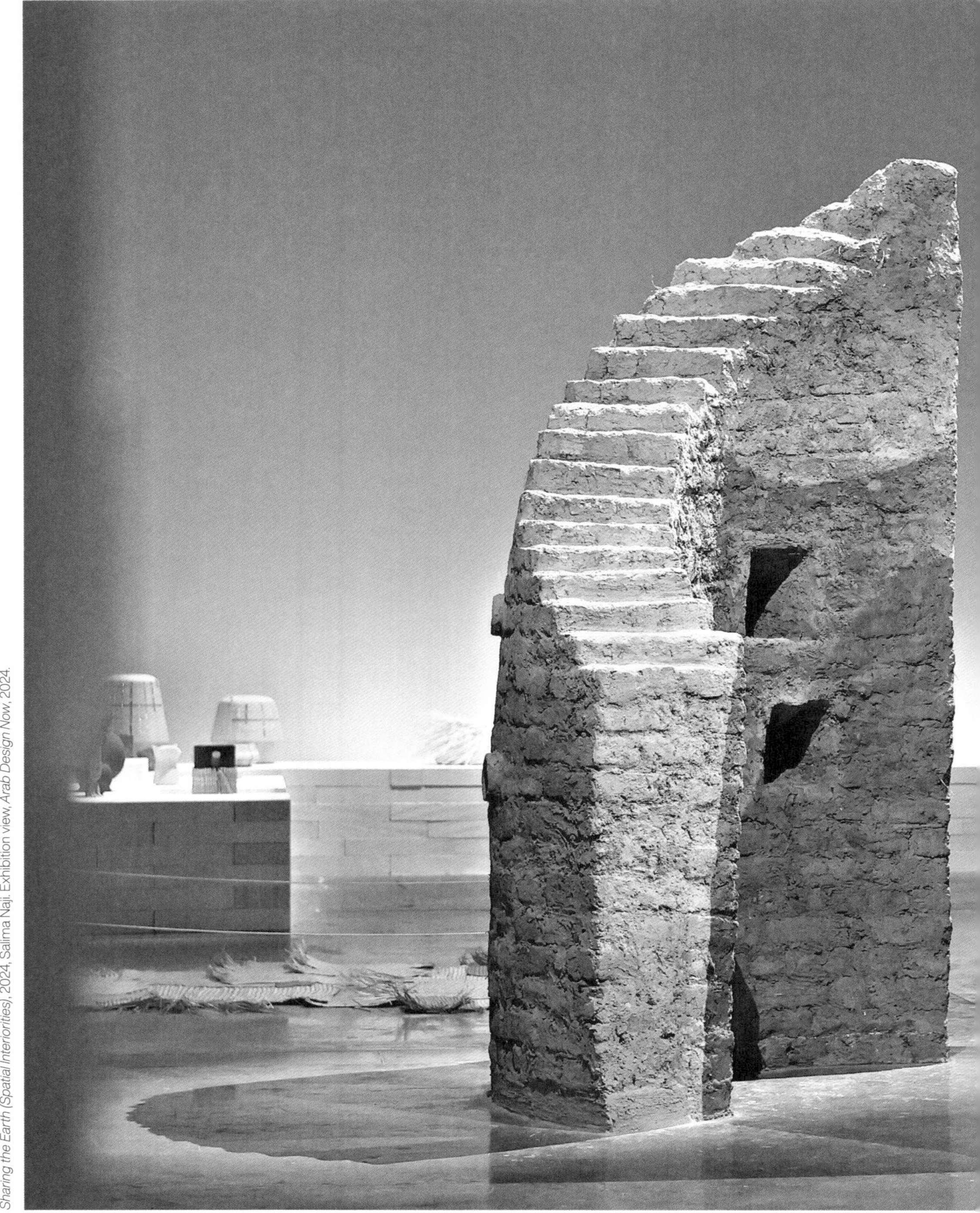

Sharing the Earth (Spatial Interiorities), 2024, Salima Naji. Exhibition view, *Arab Design Now*, 2024.

Sama El Saket

Clay in Context, 2023, Sama El Saket.

Sama El Saket is a Jordanian architect and ceramicist. Her work *Clay in Context* is a long-term research project that documents disappearing traditional ceramic techniques in Jordan and aims to uncover sites of clay harvesting by referencing geological maps, talking with craftspeople, and locating historic workshops. The resulting project features a series of vessels that present the variety of distinct clays found, harvested and processed by hand in Jordan. The repeated form references spindle storage bottles, a type produced across different periods and regions in the country, originally used to safeguard valuable oils, perfumes and medicines.

Adrian Pepe is a Beirut-based fibre artist, whose work often interweaves nature with culture, focusing on craftsmanship and performance from aesthetic, ecological and sociocultural perspectives. His tapestry, *Gilded Fleece*, is constructed from 12 discarded Awassi sheep skins, and is gilded in 24 karat gold leaf. Drawing inspiration from the theme of the Golden Fleece, one of the oldest myths of a hero's journey, the piece is a blend of tradition, innovation and critical inquiry. It invites conversations about the value and symbolism of materials, in this case gold, and of the use of domesticated animals by humans, their complex histories and cultural significance.

Adrian Pepe

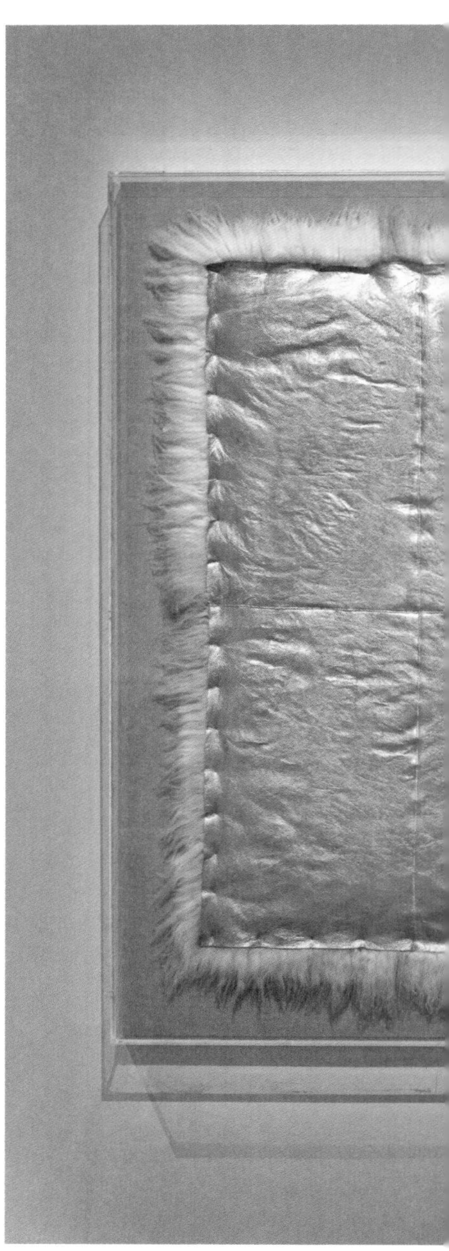

Gilded Fleece, 2024, Adrian Pepe. Exhibition view, *Arab Design Now*, 2024.

Omar Chakil

Omar 'Chakil' El Wakil is a French-Egyptian-Lebanese creative consultant, interior designer, product designer, and artist. He crafts monolithic pieces using massive blocks of Egyptian alabaster onyx carved using both mechanical methods and traditional hand crafting. His forms are inspired by multicultural and imaginative references both abstract and figurative. *Gros Guillaume Stool* alludes to a renowned 17th century French theatre actor known for his generous proportions; *Hathor* is a coffee table referencing the Ancient Egyptian goddess of beauty and maternity, among other things; and *Nubia* is a sculptural bookshelf, named after the region that connects Egypt and Sudan along the Nile River, known for its distinctive use of mud.

Left: *Gros Guillaume Stool*, 2022 and *Hathor Table*, 2023, Omar Chakil.
Above: *Nubia*, 2023, Omar Chakil.

Don Tanani is a Cairo-based Egyptian furniture design brand. The pieces designed by Lina Alorabi are crafted by skilled artisans and inspired by Ancient Egyptian gods and goddesses, patterns, and motifs, featuring hand-carving and gold leaf techniques. *Maat* is a hanging console with feather wings; *Atet* is inspired by the boat of the Egyptian god Ra, a vessel which travels to the underworld; and the gold-leafed *Shen* partition reflects on the traditional use of this material for protection.

Lina Alorabi for Don Tanani

Right: *Maat* console, Atet chair and *Shen* room divider, 2021, Lina Alorabi for Don Tanani.

"Creating in our region today is to reclaim identity and uncover lost truths and processes, including crafts that served us for millennia, and to adapt them to the present; to revive overlooked systems and redefine modernity as dependent on culture, not its replacement."

Lina Alorabi

Atet, 2021, Lina Alorabi for Don Tanani.

Nader Gammas is a lighting and furniture designer whose pieces are a symbiosis of technical performance and sculptural integrity. His work *Shard Floor Light* draws inspiration from mineral crystalline structures and features a distinctive cantilevered design comprising a base, an arm, and a light source.

Nader Gammas

•

Shard Floor Light, 2021, Nader Gammas.

Shard Floor Light, 2021, Nader Gammas.

Guided by intuition and a hands-on approach to creation, **Hozan Zangana** explores the concepts of heritage and homeland, gathering images, colours, materials, shapes and forms that inspire his sculptural works.

To me, home is both everywhere and nowhere. It is a place where I find meaning, and design purposeful things, even if they are both painful and beautiful. Home is a feeling that arises when I travel, walk and connect with kind people. It is that sense of connection that brings me solace, whether it is with a person I meet on the street or someone I encounter while taking a bus. Home is a feeling, just like any other. Everything I create stems from a feeling. I consider it a gift – being able to sense ideas and discern if a path is right for me.

I grew up in Iraq, where we constantly travelled between the Kurdish part in the North and Baghdad, my mother's hometown, which has a rich cultural landscape of artworks, sculptures and architecture. When I was 15, we moved to the Netherlands, and suddenly I found myself in a new environment with fresh perspectives. Inspired by one of my high school teachers, I pursued art, despite having no background or experience. I worked tirelessly through the night to create a portfolio and gained admission. Art school provided me with the freedom to contemplate simple things and to process the ideas and images born from my many troubling experiences – war, trauma, and other heavy burdens.

But after a year of orientation, I felt that something was missing. During a random trip to Eindhoven, I decided to trespass on its Design Academy one evening to get a glimpse of the school's atmosphere. I saw people inside preparing for a presentation and it's difficult to describe, but I felt an urgent sense, similar to what one feels in times of crisis. I knew I needed to come here and switch my major to design; and so began my fascination with shapes, materials, identity and heritage.

After graduating from the Academy and starting my own studio, I invested all my time in studying and understanding shapes – the rectangle, the triangle, the square. When and why should one use them? These simple questions became an obsession. I also dedicated much time to exploring imagery from my homeland – images of the city I had grown up in, its rooftops, architecture, mosaics and colours. Each region and village has its own unique style, patterns and shapes that blend modernity with ancient roots. I studied miniature art and sculptures from the Middle East extensively and rediscovered my childhood fascination with calligraphy, particularly the Kufic script. The ingenuity behind Kufic is truly remarkable, especially when compared to other writing systems.

Hozan Zangana

Working on my most recent object *Nahiru*, I started recognising various influences, including the Kufic script, as well as the forms and volumes of animals. I noticed similarities between my sketches and the drawings I had done from an archaeological site two years prior. I had also drawn inspiration from an ancient Egyptian sculpture depicting a hippopotamus, which I encountered at the Louvre. The hippopotamus, associated with the Goddess Taweret and referred to in ancient texts as the *faras al nahar* (seahorse), symbolises fertility and strength. This symbolism is reflected in the design of the bench, resembling a pregnant belly with its bold, voluminous shape exuding both presence and feminine softness. The hippopotamus is also known as *Nahiru* in the ancient Assyrian language, hence the name I chose for this piece.

I don't typically gather images or create mood boards intentionally; I sense forms and ideas, and consider their utility, proportions, and suitable materials. I begin with sketches, then translate them into 3D drawings, sometimes creating smaller models to refine the shape further. Once the design is complete, I revisit and reconstruct the narrative behind the object's origin. Occasionally, I subconsciously encounter a colour or shape, and weeks later I'll rediscover it manifesting in my work. I always carry my sketchbook with me, ready to capture any ideas that come my way. It's like fishing, where one must remain prepared and alert for any opportunities. Each day is an unknown catch, but I have faith in the process. It's fascinating how the brain works subconsciously, constantly making connections and associations without our awareness. I compare it to movie-making; I may have only glimpsed a frame or two, but I strive to piece everything together to create a complete film.

The artwork *Kisal*, for example, is a captivating sculptural calligraphy piece that embodies the narrative of the region. Inspired by the tortoise, the name holds symbolic significance from various chronological contexts. Throughout history, the tortoise has represented resistance and endurance, serving as a metaphorical wellspring of strength. *Kisal* showcases the influence of Mesopotamic and Assyrian narratives, symbolising the preservation of cultural heritage and resilience within ancient cultures, reminding us of our innate capacity to adapt and triumph over adversity.

Above: Hippopotamus amulet, Predynastic, Naqada I–early Naqada II, c. 3700–3450 B.C., Egypt. Collection of the Metropolitan Museum of Art, New York. Right: *Nahiru Bench*, 2020, Hozan Zangana.

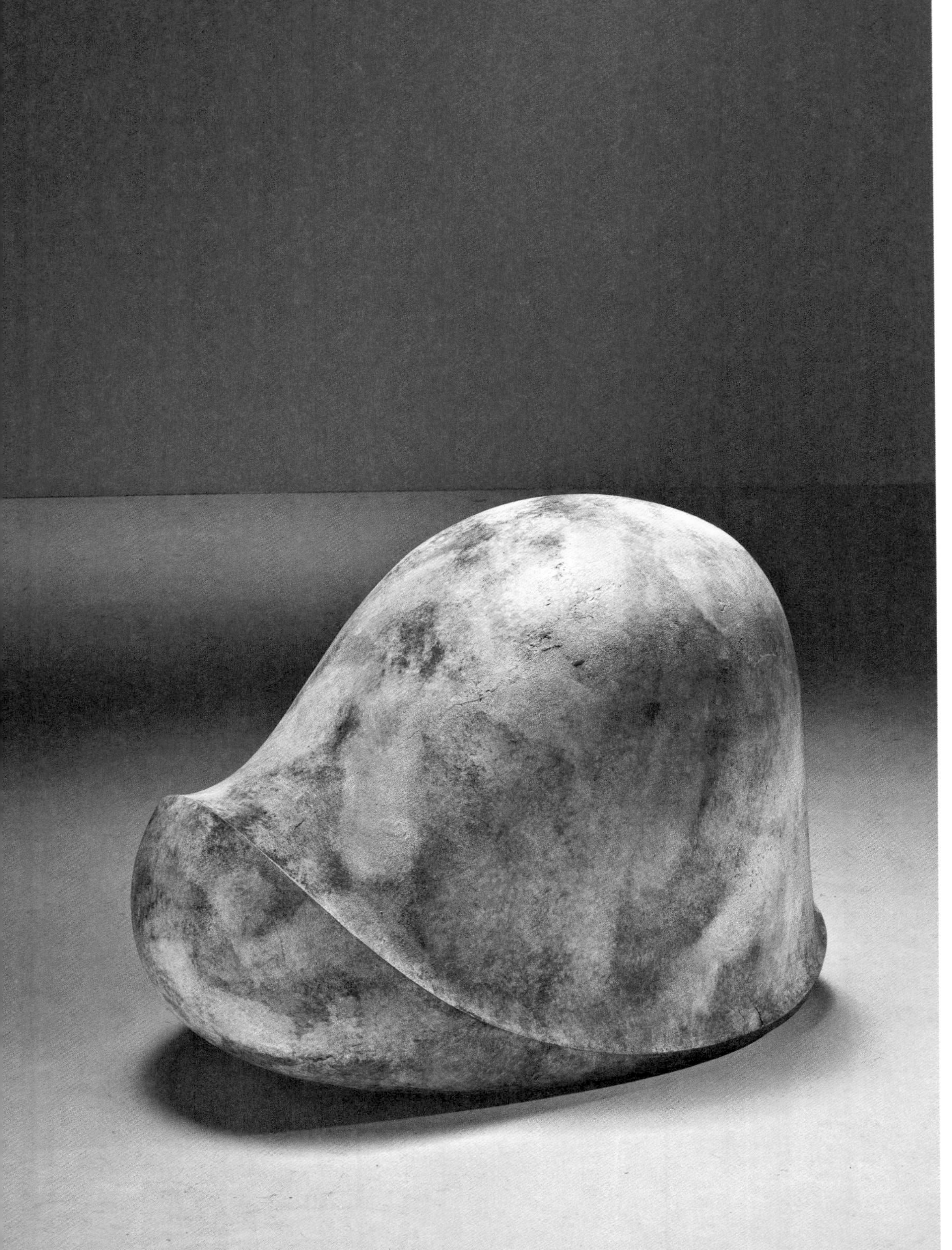

Sculpture holds a significant place in my body of work, evolving from intuitive inspiration through various iterations. *Kisal* takes on a unique voluminous form – not precisely round – and has undergone notable developments, resulting in 13 versions. Just like calligraphy, each line and letter carries its own significance and distinction. The crafting demands careful consideration and materials that align with the intended message. Creating a single line can be a meticulous process, often taking hours of patience and refinement. While it may seem impossible at first, it eventually materialises effortlessly after a restful night's sleep. Yet, even when satisfied, the piece is never truly complete, leaving room for future exploration. Knowing when to pause and engage with the craftsman is another fascinating aspect of the creative journey.

During the 2019 *Arbela* exhibition in the Kurdish capital Erbil, where we were happy to see the collection go to the home of its inspiration, I embarked on a new version of *Kisal*. I extensively experimented with its patina, reimagining it in diverse colours such as gold, red and silver. Colours significantly influence the perception of an object. Grey may cause it to fade into the background, whereas red imparts a greater sense of significance. The colour choice depends on the concept and the desired emotional response. Understanding the project's essence and the intended message is crucial. For this reason, I utilised a patina to infuse the wood with reddish-brown tones reminiscent of sandstorms in the Middle East. In another instance, we sought to establish a connection to calligraphy, applying 16 layers of East-Indian ink to the object *Hunebench*, each layer meticulously polished. Although the process demanded extensive effort, I relished the joy of experimentation, embracing the uncertainty of the final outcome. To this day, we remain unaware of how it will respond to time and the environment. Yet, in my view, this ambiguity adds value and richness to the piece.

Whenever we embark on a new project, we prioritise the use of local materials and craftsmanship. I dedicate months to experimentation and creating models, immersing myself in a process of deep obsession, seeking a profound connection between heritage and the choice of material. When creating *Brinkei Nabinraw*, for example, I carefully considered the message I wanted

Left: *Kisal Stool*, 2024, Hozan Zangana. Below: Tortoise figurine, early Bronze Age, c. late 3rd millennium BCE, Mesopotamia, Tell Taya. Collection of the Metropolitan Museum of Art, New York.

to convey. Wood or bronze didn't resonate as strongly as recycled plastic in accurately representing the way refugees are often perceived—individuals without status or political power, dehumanised and easily disregarded by the world.

Wood holds a special place in my work, as I'm captivated by its living nature and rich historical significance. However, working with wood poses considerable challenges, particularly when aiming for sharp lines and distinct shapes. Unlike stone for example, wood undergoes transformations over time due to factors like air temperature and humidity. I find it fascinating that even after an object's completion, wood continues to evolve, keeping it alive.

In my recent endeavours, I have delved into the realm of lacquer, collaborating with craftsmen from the Akita and Echizen prefectures in Japan. This intricate material presents technical complexities and allergenic properties that make personal experimentation challenging for me. To overcome this, I have joined forces with my talented friend and craftsman Dave van Gompel to develop a technique that merges my designs and signature with

Left: Works by Hozan Zangana displayed in Expo Erbil/Hawler, Kurdistan Iraq, 2019. Right: *Qalat Hunebench*, 2016, Hozan Zangana, displayed in Milan curated Stef Bakker, 2016.

the essence of lacquer. I recognise that mastery of this material demands extensive time and dedication to achieve the desired shape and perfection.

Building positive and constructive relationships with skilled craftsmen profoundly impacts my work and I greatly value the relationships I establish with them, many of whom I have known for years. Their expertise and input play a vital role in bringing my designs to life. Often, these craftsmen propose alternative approaches that prove simpler and more effective than my initial ideas. As a result, I don't consider myself the sole creator with the final say. My designs remain open to their input, and I view them as shared endeavours rather than solely my own. It is akin to channelling ideas and manifesting them, hoping that others will appreciate and enjoy the final outcome — a parallel to the act of fishing.

At times, it is beneficial to revert to the role of a student. I don't confine myself strictly to being a designer or artist who must always maintain control. I have a genuine desire to continuously learn and deepen my understanding across various subjects. Therefore, I occasionally reach out to individuals who inspire me, and offer my assistance on their projects. This approach allows me to forge connections, embrace new challenges, and explore without the pressure of specific outcomes.

In our studio, each project we embark on is a celebration of our heritage and diverse backgrounds. With a partnership spanning 22 years, my wife Niloufar and I bring our unique strengths to the table. She excels in planning, organising and management, while I pour my passion into design. Together, we create a dynamic synergy that brings our visions to life. Beyond our professional collaboration, our family embodies the beauty of cultural fusion. Our children are a wonderful blend of languages and backgrounds, forming a tapestry of diversity and richness. Their unique perspectives and experiences add vibrant colours to our lives. We cherish and embrace this mosaic, as it reminds us of the importance of unity and love across borders.

Our work is driven by the imperative to protect our heritage, language and manuscripts. In times of conflict and upheaval, the destruction of cultural identity emerges as a primary target. The loss of significant cultural artefacts, such as the Bamiyan Buddha

sculptures in Afghanistan or the sculptures in Nimrud and Nineveh in Iraq, deeply resonates as a collective trauma. This loss extends beyond specific regions; it affects us all. We firmly believe that safeguarding sculptures, language, rituals and storytelling is vital for preserving the spirit and collective identity of a people. Through the recreation or creation of new artistic expressions, whether through paintings, movies or other mediums, we breathe life into the narratives of our heritage – Assyrian, Egyptian, Babylonian – and ensure their enduring presence. Preserving what we cherish ultimately saves us and connects us to ourselves and each other.

Pain knows no boundaries, and artworks transcend time, binding us together as part of our shared human history. It is a heritage that belongs to all of us, not just one person.

For my current collection, inspiration struck when I watched a short film titled *Al Zubarah* in Qatar. The well-preserved fortified town that thrived as a trading and pearling centre in the 18th and 19th centuries features extensive ruins, including houses, mosques, and a defensive wall, providing insights into the town's urban layout and social organisation. The aerial shots showcasing the vastness of the land and sky left an indelible impression. This experience ignited a creative exploration of colours, textures, and the development of a new patina.

In contrast to my previous inclination towards smooth perfection, which may have been shaped by my origins in a tumultuous and fragmented place, I have learned to appreciate the beauty of imperfection. Just like the sight of an old car in the Middle East, where plastic wrap clings to worn-out seats, there is a certain charm in the weathered and damaged. With age, our own skin becomes marked by the passage of time, acquiring character and resilience. It is this very roughness that now captivates me, compelling me to delve into the stories that completed objects hold. I am driven by a profound desire to unravel their narratives and discover the unique essence they possess. It is through these imperfections that these pieces come alive, exuding a magnetic allure that resonates deep within, infusing them with soulful significance.

Works by Hozan Zangana displayed in Milan curated Stef Bakker, 2016.

Left: *Hapiru Stool*, 2024, Hozan Zangana. Right: Hozan Zangana working in his studio.

Hozan Zangana is a Kirkuk-born artist and designer living in the Netherlands. His sculptural furniture engages with a wide range of materials, techniques, collaborations and contexts. His practice is heritage-driven and draws inspiration from ancient sculptures, language, traditions and rituals. His works, the *Nahiru Bench,* the *Kisal Stool* and the *Hapiru Stool,* reference ancient Assyrian and Mesopotamian animal motifs and artefacts.

Sizar Alexis is a Swedish-Iraqi designer. Through his works, which are inspired by the rich architectural heritage of ancient Mesopotamia, he explores his own identity and position as a designer within the Chaldean diaspora. Alongside his use of raw and inherently beautiful natural materials, he imbues his pieces with a sense of stillness, serenity and strength by using solid geometrical shapes. His sculptural furniture includes a chair and stool set, named *Ousia*, which he made in collaboration with his sister Sinar Alexis, and the bunker-inspired *Lahmu*, a monumental piece made of burned and stained black solid oak.

Ousia, 2022, Sizar and Sinar Alexis.

Sizar Alexis

Lahmu, 2022, Sizar Alexis.

Samer Selbak is a Paris-based Palestinian artist and designer. His work questions the relationship between humans and nature with the intention of bringing them closer together, while reviving and repurposing natural materials. The *Reef* space divider and *Saffeer* pendant lamps are crafted from dyed luffa fibres, which have been treated, shaped, flattened and sewn. The resilient and biodegradable plant fibre permits air and light to pass through, giving them an almost mystical presence. The pieces are supported by steel armatures, which simultaneously are elements of both form and function.

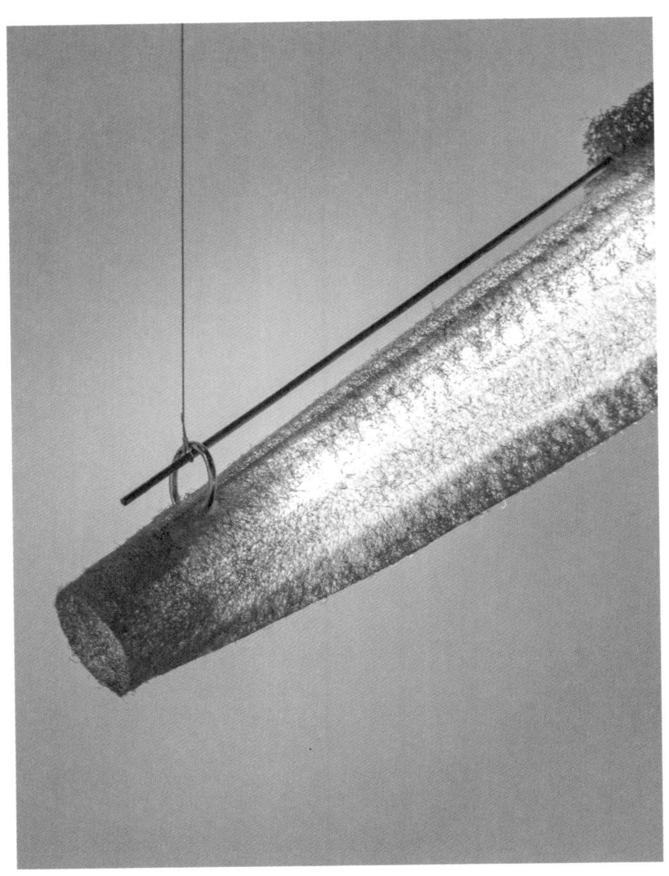

Reef and *Saffeer*, 2022, Samer Selbak. Exhibition view, *Arab Design Now*, 2014.

Samer Selbak

Abeer Seikaly

Abeer Seikaly is a Jordanian-Palestinian artist, architect and designer. Her practice centres indigenous Bedouin knowledge to recover the intimacy of hand making. In *Constellations 2.0: Object. Light. Consciousness.*, Abeer draws upon heritage from Italy and her Arab homeland, merging Venetian glassmaking and Bedouin weaving. The resulting suspended light sculpture is handcrafted from over 5000 pieces of Murano glass. When illuminated, it generates cosmological patterns of light and movement.

Constellations 2.0: Object. Light. Consciousness., 2023, Abeer Seikaly.

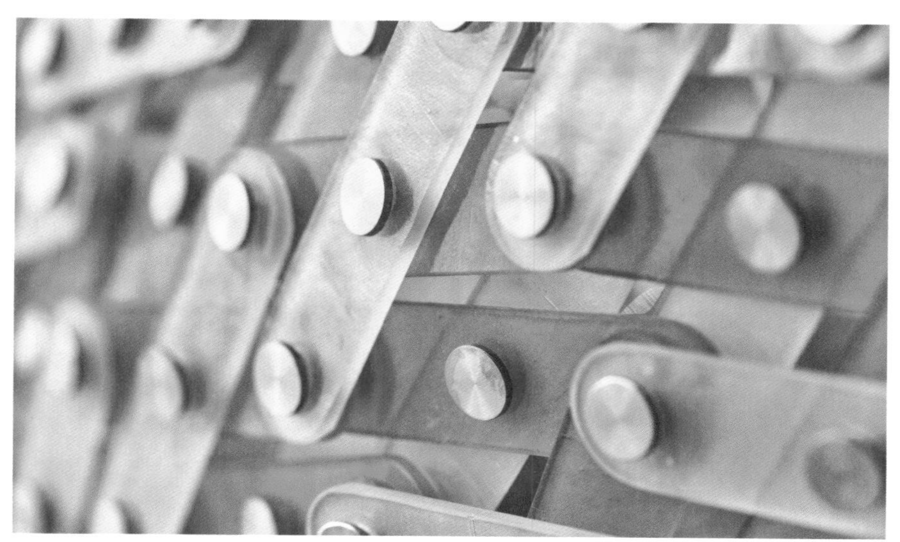

Constellations 2.0: Object. Light. Consciousness, 2023, Abeer Seikaly. Exhibition view, *Arab Design Now*, 2024.

Reverie, 2024, Hiba Shahzada.
Exhibition view, *Arab Design Now*, 2024.

Hiba Shahzada is an Amman-based architect and artist. She explores the possibility of new affiliations between art and architecture, often making paintings of spaces before translating them into reality. Her indoor water pavilion, *Reverie*, features a suspended wooden ceiling with a domed faceted interior, and floats above four free standing wooden pillars set directly in a reflecting pool. Evoking the common traditional architectural typology of the fountain, the resulting pavilion offers a place of respite, pause, wonder and renewal.

Hiba Shahzada

"To create something meaningful means to work with the strengths and ambitions of craftsmen born into a heritage of traditional yet visionary trades, and to work with our varied landscapes, majestic and enduring, and unforgiving, while reaching for novelty, in beauty and precision, as it once had overflowed from the region."

Hiba Shahzada

Reverie, 2024, Hiba Shahzada. Exhibition view, *Arab Design Now*, 2024.

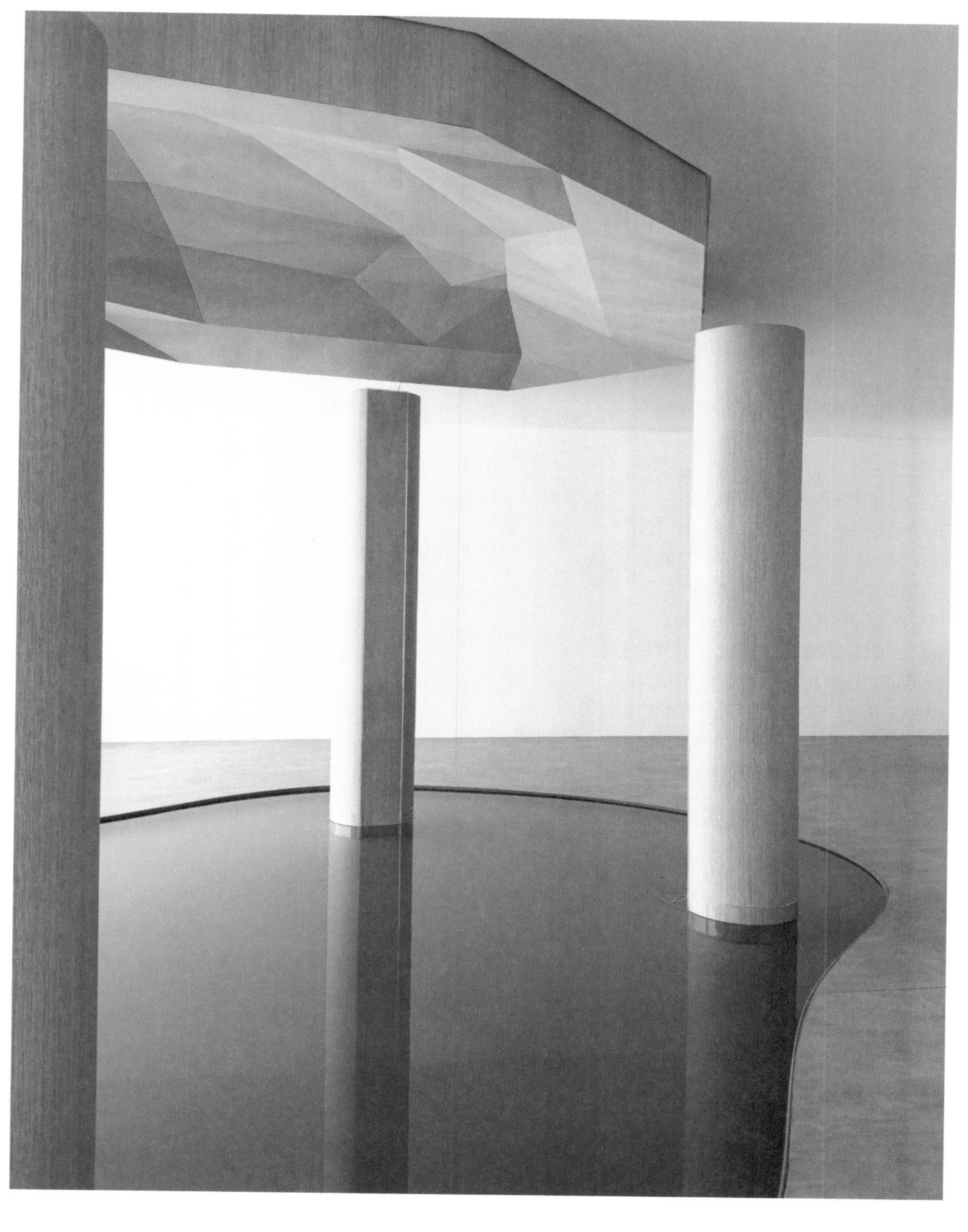

NEW SOUTH

NEW SOUTH is an international architecture studio based in Paris, focused on engaging with contested territories, vulnerable bodies and sacred spaces. Their installation *Kursi* is an ambiguous sacred space, in which they reflect on the specificities of mosque design in non-Muslim majority contexts. The installation suggests various ways of creating a sanctuary. Using furniture as the basis for this exploration, simple stools can be placed together or scattered around the space. Spread out or aligned, single or stacked, the geometrically shaped ceramic stools can potentially create a multitude of worlds.

Kursi, 2024, New South. Exhibition view, *Arab Design Now*, 2024.

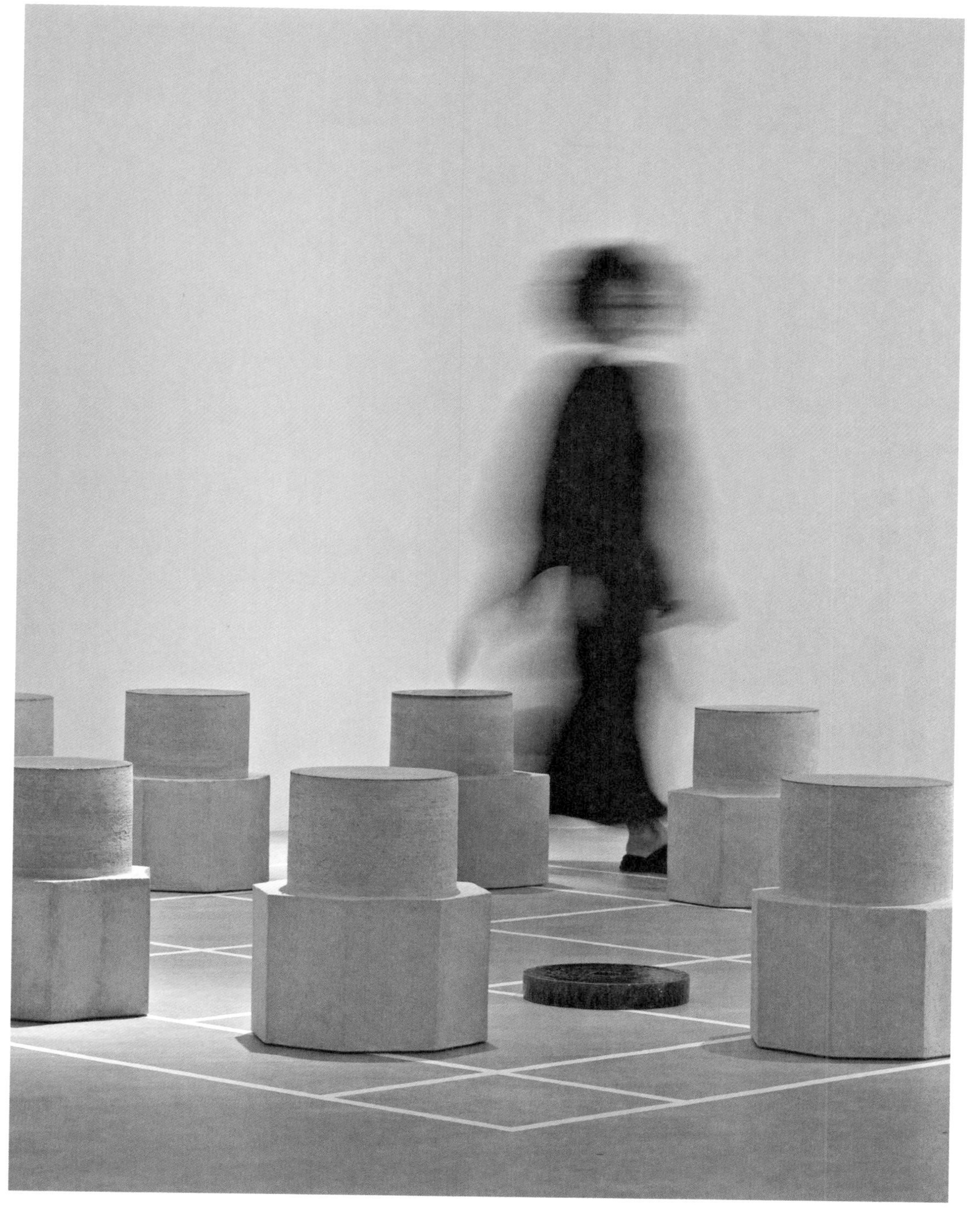

“In the region, as anywhere, we don’t create, we give voice to what is already there.”

Meriem Chabani and John Edom

Kursi, 2024, New South. Exhibition view, *Arab Design Now*, 2024.

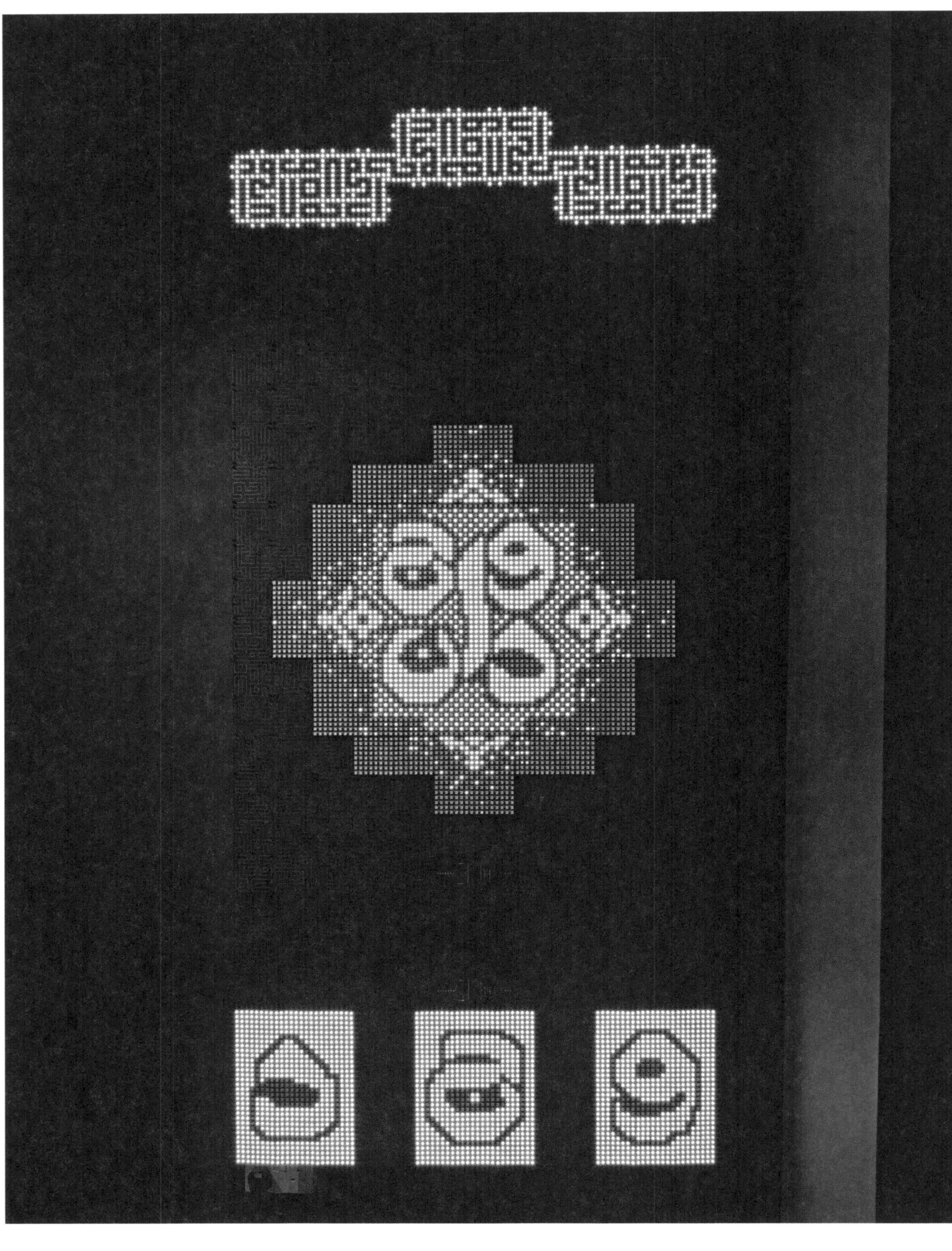

TypeAraby and xLab

TypeAraby and xLab, represented by Basma Hamdy and Levi Hammett respectively, are part of the Institute for Creative Research at Virginia Commonwealth University School of the Arts in Qatar. Merging the study of Arabic script, design and visual culture, and the synthesis of computational processes and traditional crafts, the two teams collaborated to produce this animated electronic tapestry. The piece reflects on the words *Wujood*, meaning existence, *Wijdan*, meaning awareness or consciousness, and their trilateral root *Wajad*. The work serves as a visual ode to the three-letter root system at the core of the Arabic language and script, and reflects on how technological constraints sometimes cause a loss of spiritual resonance.

Wujood, 2024, TypeAraby & xLab, Institute for Creative Research, Virginia Commonwealth University School of the Arts in Qatar. Exhibition view, *Arab Design Now*, 2024.

Fabraca Studios

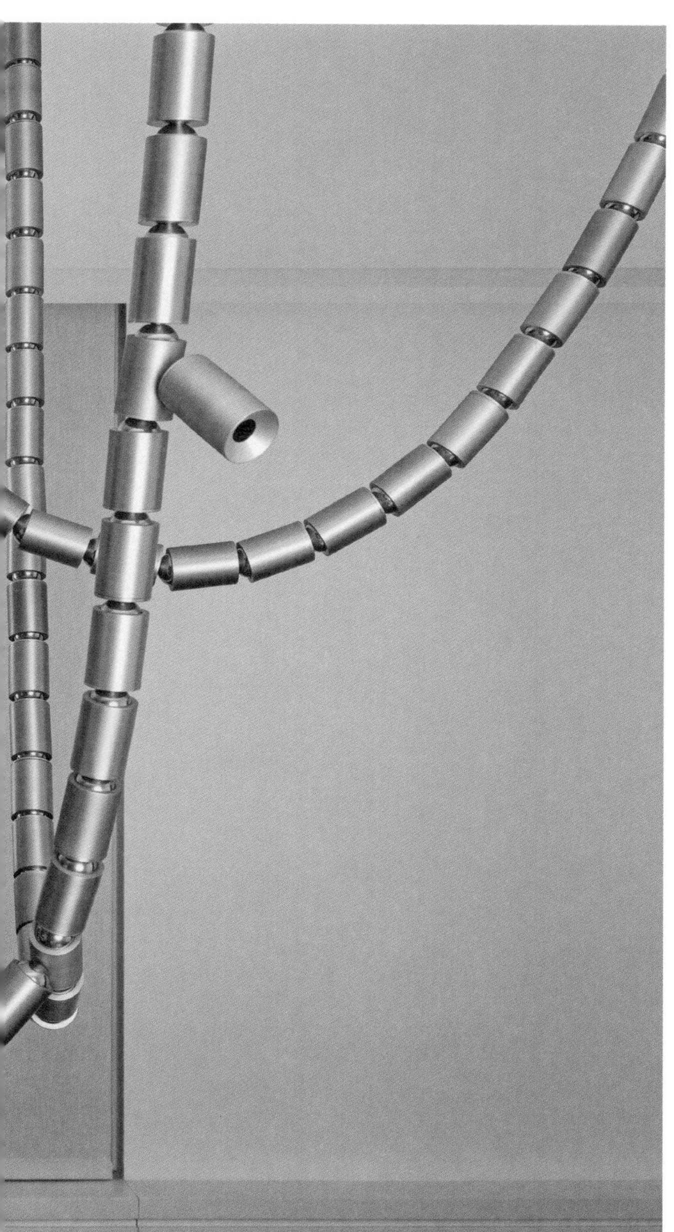

Fabraca Studios is a Beirut-based team of architects, engineers and artists. Their lighting projects blend modern design and modularity with local craftsmanship in an effort to revive traditional skills. *Light Impact* is a particularly unique chandelier, originally commissioned to replace a fixture that was destroyed in the aftermath of the 2020 Beirut explosion. Located at a vantage point overlooking the blast site and guided by the principle that 'what bends doesn't break', the aim was to create a flexible and enduring lighting fixture, resilient against future shocks. The modular piece is composed of interconnected aluminium cylinders, evoking the appearance of a rope.

Light Impact, 2022, Fabraca Studios.

Light Impact, 2022, Fabraca Studios.

Ali Kaaf

Ali Kaaf is an Algerian-born Syrian visual artist based in Berlin. His work spans a diversity of mediums including blown glass sculpture, installations, film and painting. The *Helmet* series is a collection of sculptures inspired by ancient military headgear from a diversity of historical moments. Despite being used by fighters of different cultures and across time, these helmets often share the same destiny, becoming relics in museums. For the artist, the choice of material adds fragility to an object that remains resilient throughout history, unlike the humans it served to protect.

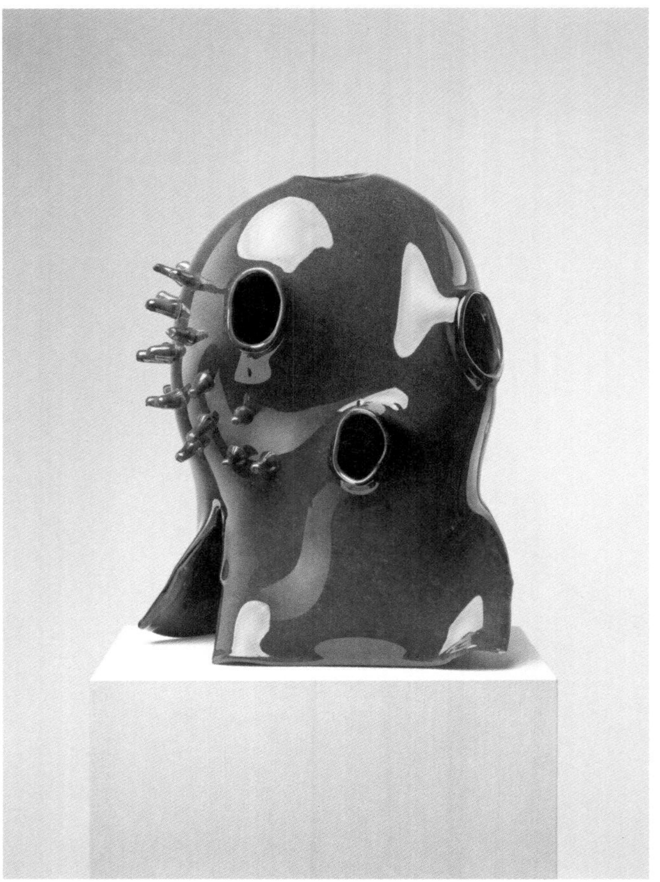

Helmet, 2024, Ali Kaaf.

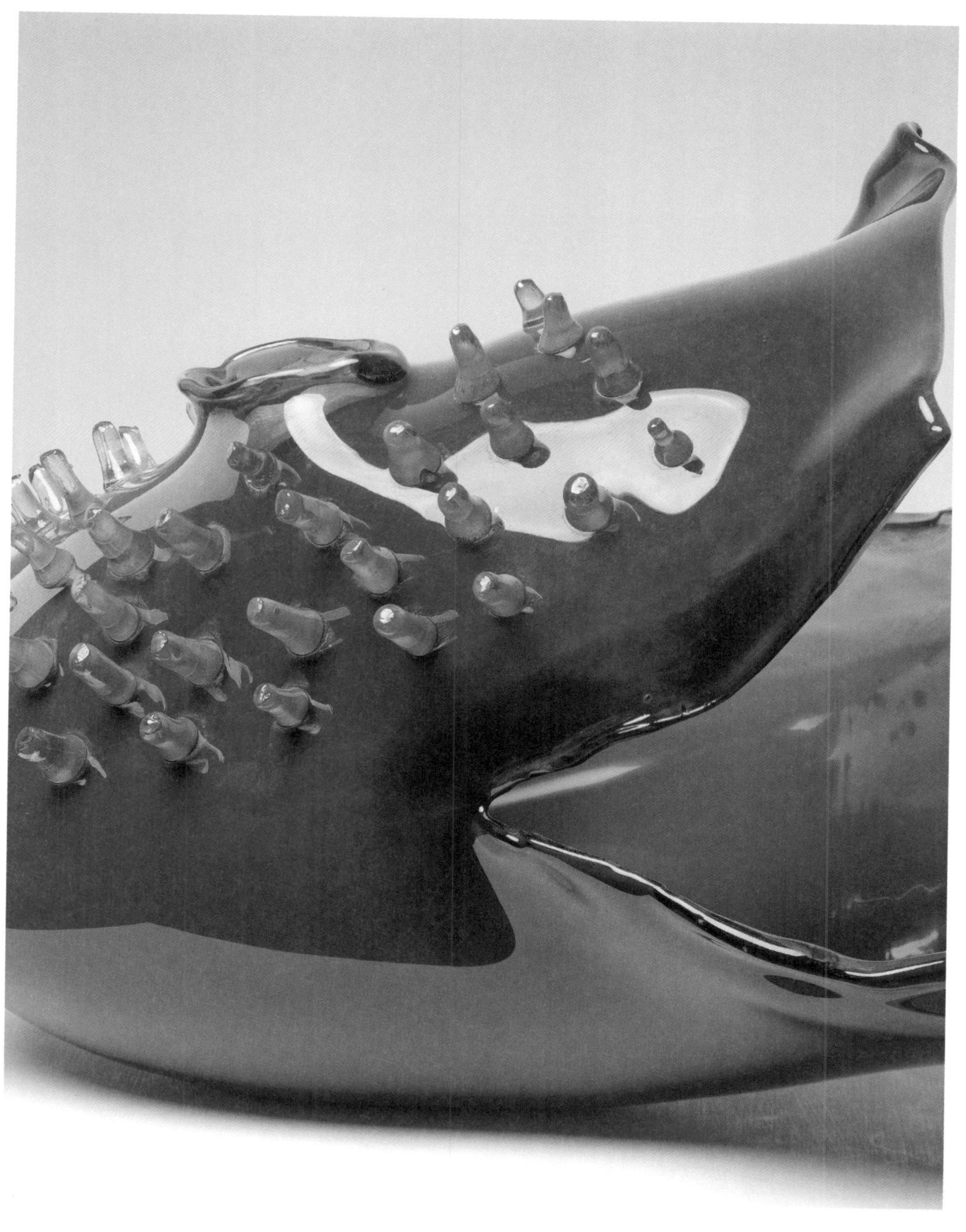

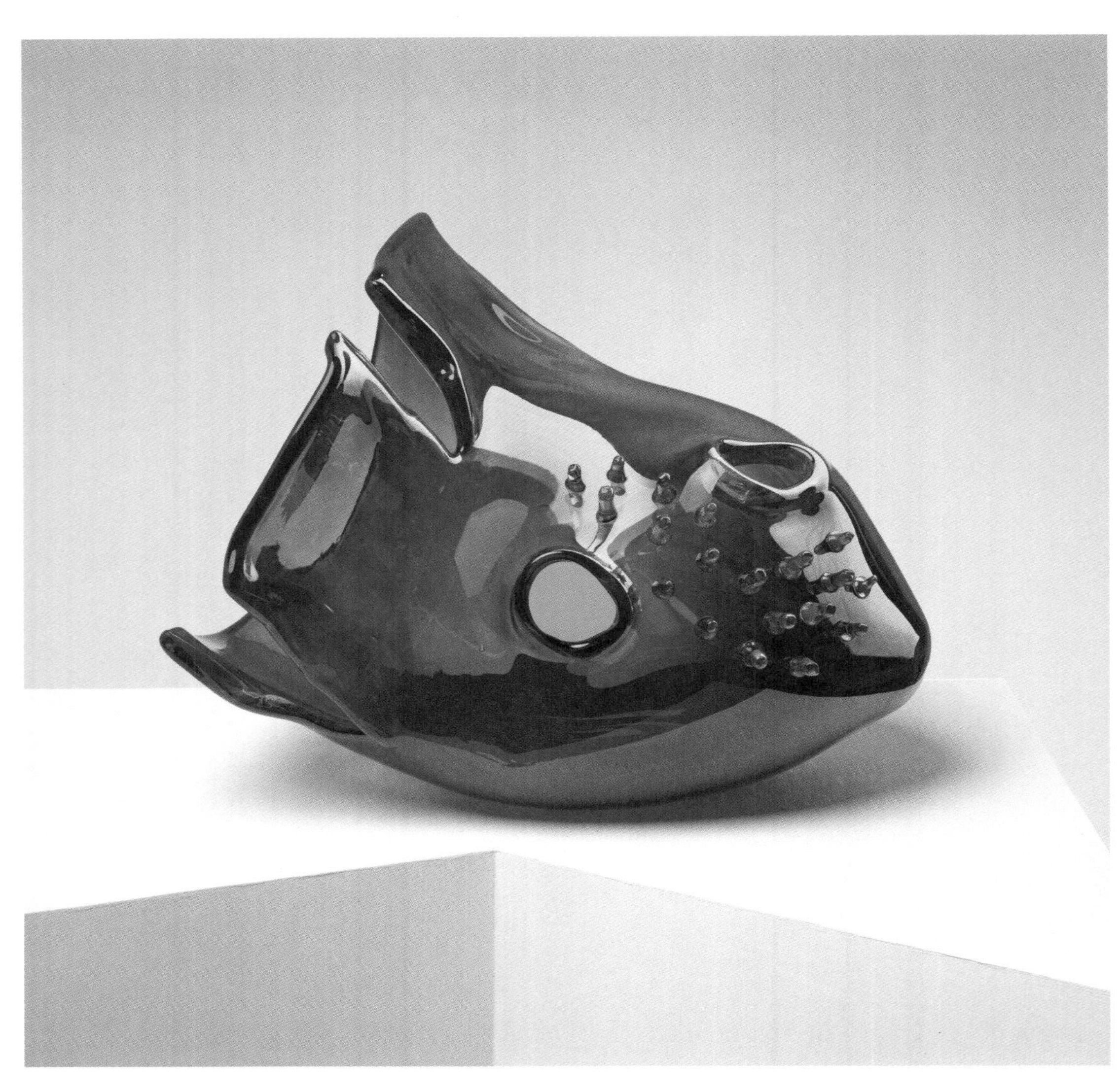

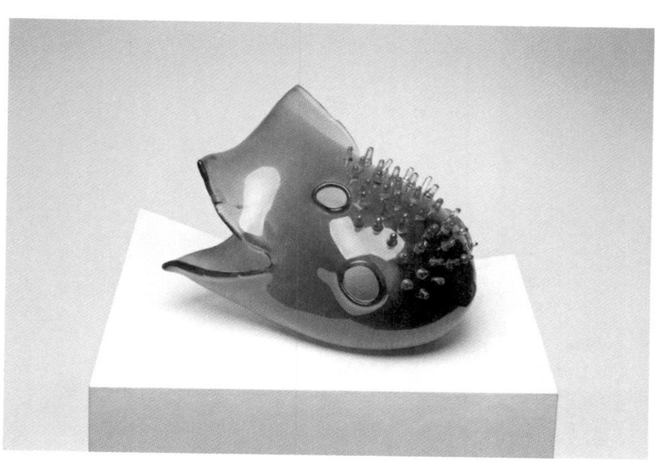

Helmet, 2024, Ali Kaaf.

T SAKHI

T SAKHI is a multidisciplinary architecture and design studio cofounded by Lebanese-Polish sisters Tessa and Tara El Sakhi. Their projects range from collectible objects to small-scale architecture, commercial and residential interior design, scenography and urban installations. The installation *Whispers from the Deep* is composed of translucent metal-infused glass vessels reminiscent of underwater sea creatures. Crafted in Murano, an epicentre of glassmaking for centuries, the pieces draw connections and shared knowledge between Venetian artisans and the glassblowing heritage in Lebanon, tracing back to the Phoenicians from across the Mediterranean.

Whispers from the Deep, 2024, T SAKHI.
Photos by Lorenzo Basadonna Scarpa.

Exhibition view, *Arab Design Now*, 2024.

In their various research-based projects, architects **Elias** and **Yousef Anastas** revive the use of structural stone in building, with a deep and careful consideration of notions such as territory, building process, and form.

The act of building, by itself, is a beautiful process that blends know-how, cultural resources, climatic conditions and ways of living. It is, in many ways, almost a primitive act.

In Palestine, the most common construction material is stone. Stone is abundant, widely available and, perhaps most importantly, thanks to an urban law imposed by the British Mandate legally required in construction for the purpose of creating a unified language in the built environment. This type of law underlines a shift from a self-managed urbanism, which used stone as a building material, to an authority-based urbanism which results in a 'dwarfed' use of stone as simply a material for cladding. This 'misuse' of stone compromises its structural qualities, in favour of a more contemporary aesthetic, leading to the disappearance of historic stone-building know-how and techniques. This, of course, was further compounded by the emergence of reinforced concrete in the 1940s and 1950s, resulting in further loss of the craft.

As a reaction to the systematic misuse of cladding stone in Palestine, we began producing a series of interactive projects linked under an experimentation-based research umbrella we called *Stone Matters*. Evolving over the past 10 years, we have experimented with 1:1 scale prototypes and site-specific constructions, including a vault, a lintel, a slab, a wall, a column, and so on. The scale of each project always corresponds to the context of a building and takes its cues from the historic recurrence of stone-made architectural elements found in Palestine.

The recognition of the persistence of stone's significance in Palestinian cityscapes, while also accounting for the radical shifts in the use of the material, has become the central spine along which we built our practice. Therefore, our work often references and investigates the taxonomy of elements from disparate influences that have been brought to Palestinian cities by various civilisations, as well as those elements of local origin. While stone is often associated exclusively with noble or holy constructions, we attempt to 'desacralise' it by creating a wide vocabulary of stone use to encourage its inclusion in various forms of contemporary architecture.

In the different experimentations under *Stone Matters*, two simultaneous efforts take place, where defining the process is as important and time-consuming as defining the form. Whether it's a prototype, a small building, a part of a building, or a pavilion, the form is not just a product of studying the capabilities of stone, or how it behaves structurally, or how much weight it can withstand. Each form is born out of a specific site condition or cultural condition, and responds to an identified need or function. It's about how to push techniques beyond boundaries, or pushing the material itself beyond its limits, while at the same time trying to respond formally and in a basic way to the architectural need.

One of our earliest experiments, for example, was to design the pavilion for the el-Atlal artists' and writers' residency in the Palestinian city of Jericho. We were collaborating with a very young institution that didn't really have the means to fund a large scale project, so building with economy was an important factor. The project became an architectural prototype and case study.

We, of course, started with the question: 'What does it mean to create a cultural program in a city that is largely culturally marginalised?' Since Jericho is mostly a flat topography, we wanted to create something that resonates with the movement of the wind, and to create a structure that truly breathes.

Bottom left: *The Stonesourcing Space*, 2012, Bethlehem, AAU Anastas. Below and bottom right: *Stone Matters Vault*, 2017, for the el-Atlal residency in Jericho, AAU Anastas.

While stone is a dominant building material in Palestine, it had become less visible in Jericho over the past 50 years. More recently however, in the last 15 to 20 years, stone has been reintroduced in a very stylistic and folkloric way that is very disconnected from the city itself. So we were faced with the challenge of introducing a material and construction principle to the city in a way that is relevant to the existing urbanism. The final form was a porous space consisting of 12 interconnected stone vaults.

A major problem we have, which is common in different parts of the Middle East, is that heritage preservation is limited to a certain framework. In Palestine, buildings constructed after the 1920s are not considered heritage buildings, while in reality, some of the buildings from the 1940s and 1950s have architectural features and elements that are way more fragile and interesting than those that are preserved under law. It creates a distorted lens on history, where a specific subset is allowed to be demolished. We wanted to explore an expanded idea of preservation by looking at salvaged stone from these demolished buildings and how it can be recycled. These structural stones have dimensions that used to carry entire buildings, so when you recycle them, they offer many possibilities.

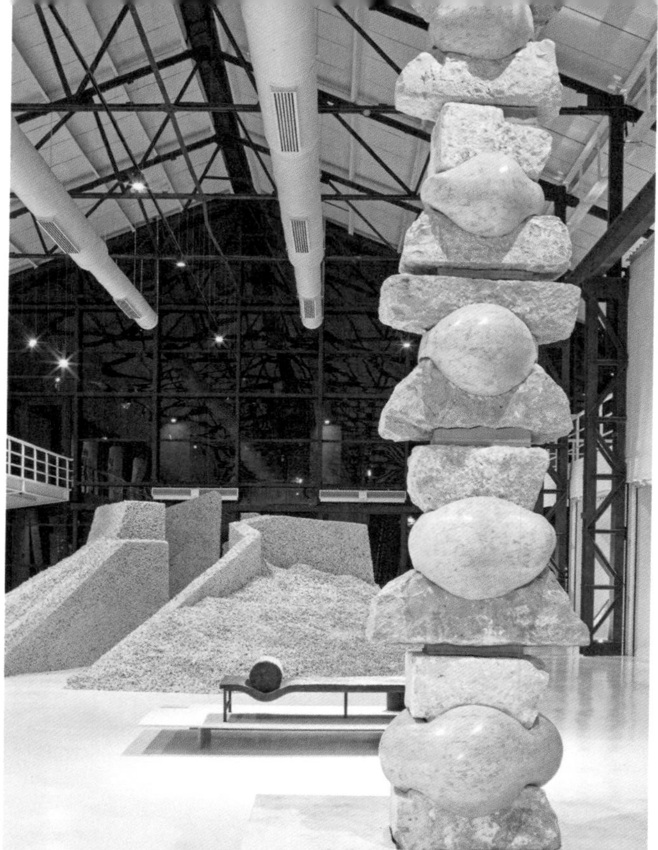

Amoud, 2019, AAU Anastas. Exhibition view, Amman Design Week, 2019.

With the stone ruins, we created a piece called *Amoud* for Amman Design Week. It is a column made out of different stone elements that come from different periods and illustrate different construction techniques. The collected stones were geometrically analysed, each with its unique interface, to allow us to create a self-standing massive stone column. As an installation, it addresses a global question on the re-use of salvaged building components and their adaptations into new forms of contemporary architecture.

Our projects for *Stone Matters* are constantly nourished by site specific conditions at different scales – territorial limitations, natural and urban environments, and historical contexts – and our method always originates from notions of territory; whether it's the act of marking property to the use of salvaged stone from demolished buildings. In the piece *While We Wait*, for example, which was commissioned by the Victoria and Albert Museum and exhibited during the 2017 London Design Festival, we were reacting to the cultural and territorial claim over nature in Palestine. Historically, Palestinians have always had a strong attachment to their land, and the belief that the land is sacred. Architectural forms in Palestine are often defined by the idea of preserving territory, and also by the unique topography that characterises many Palestinian cities. As a result, the urban morphology of cities is often based on a duality between a very dense nucleus at the centre, and the periphery being intentionally left untouched. The project *While We Wait*, was thus conceived on the idea of mimicking the topography and contour lines of the valley. Structurally it relies on the different concave and circular forms of the stone bricks. The installation is composed of pieces of stone quarried in various regions of Palestine, which fit together to form a large, lattice-like, self-supporting structure using principles of stereotomy, the art of cutting stones for assembly. As such, the stone pieces interlock in a way that once they are placed and surrounded by neighbouring pieces, they can no longer be removed. It is an architectural work that is there simply to mark the property in an area that is eminently being exposed to expropriation.

The evolution of stone construction in Palestine is a marker of transitions in urban and social structures, and narrates the evolution of the morphology of Palestinian cities. Through time, certain architectural attributes that were originally found and produced locally have inspired building practices abroad, which were then once again returned to Palestine. They were falsely labelled as 'imported' architectural elements. When architectural forms born from a specific cultural context are imported to another location, they get absorbed into the local context and transformed by local forms of knowledge and materials. This creates a much more vibrant idea of how cultures can be connected, without trying to read the architecture in a supremacist way.

Our latest series of projects, titled *Analogy*, address this recurrence of stone-made forms and spatial configurations in Palestine through time. *Analogy* explores the inherent qualities of fundamental architectural elements, such as vaults, lintels and columns, and aims to find novel ways of expressing each. The project started when we were looking at the cupola of the Church of Saint Anne in Jerusalem, which was built by the Crusaders. Then one day, we discovered that there's an Abbey in France that has a strikingly similar cupola to this church, and was built using similar construction techniques, also by the Crusaders, but after the one in Jerusalem. So we had the idea to look at the analogies between these two structures and try to analyse what was actually brought by the Crusaders at that time to Palestine, and then try to import this knowledge to create an extension to the Abbaye de Boschaud in France, which we were commissioned to build.

Another project we did, under *Analogy*, presents a vault inspired by a typology used in Islamic architecture since the Mamluk dynasty (13th century) and was continuously employed through different configurations, such as in the palaces of the Renaissance, as well as in common houses during the Ottoman period. For the project, we studied stone lintels in Palestine with fine interface carving, dating back to the beginning of

While We Wait, 2017, Cremisan Valley, AAU Anastas.

AAU ANASTAS

last century, and took stock of the processes, tools, techniques, and time spans, which are still all debatable. *Aqd Takaneh*, as the piece is called, consists of stone *voussoirs* that support each other relying on stereotomy, inspired by several lintels and vaults found in Jerusalem. The structure was unveiled at the Lutheran School in Jerusalem during the Jerusalem Show as part of the Qalandiya International Biennial in 2018.

Later, when we were approached by the Victoria and Albert Museum to make a piece for their collection, we became very interested in the different structural stone lintels found at the museum itself. Inspired by stereotomy found in the lintels of the Old City of Jerusalem, we created *Qamt*, a circular lintel bench, which serves as a functional structure as well as an illustrative fundamental architectural element. The piece relies only on the friction of the interfaces to stand by itself.

Above all, *Stone Matters* looks with hindsight at the history of stone architecture in order to better expand the possibilities of building with stone today. Our latest iteration, *Tiamat*, brings together intrinsic geometrical properties of surfaces inspired by the ridges of sand dunes, ribbed structures and vaulted systems. The piece looks more widely at combining techniques, forms, theoretical and/or natural principles to suggest new ways of using stone in contemporary architecture.

The geometry of *Tiamat* relies on medial axes and constant slope surfaces. These types of surfaces are remarkable because their slope, at any point, remains constant with respect to a reference plane. It can be best imaged as sand dunes, where a grain of sand placed on a pile of sand rolls and slides along a consistent sloped line. The ridges formed by this constant rolling are called the 'skeleton' of the surface. *Tiamat's* global geometry, therefore, is built around a constant slope surface whose main ridge and secondary ridges are remarkable opportunities to act as structural ribs. The structure combines geometrical properties, Gothic-inspired structural systems and pointed arches found across Palestine, Syria and Lebanon.

Above: *Analogy*, 2018, AAU Anastas. Jerusalem Show IX. Right: *Qamt*, 2019, AAU Anastas. V&A Museum, London.

AAU ANASTAS

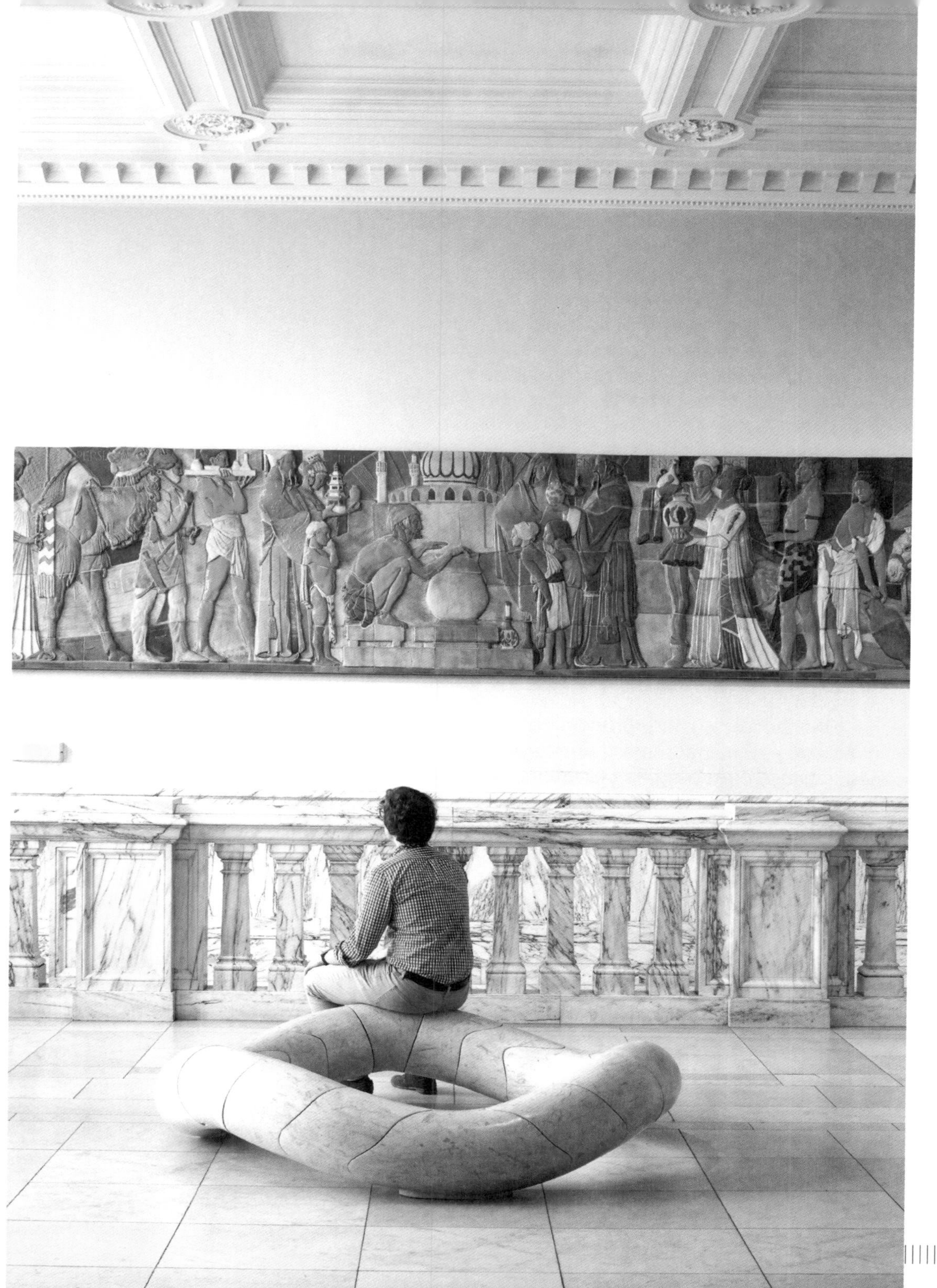

Within the cavity is a unique architectural space that creates the essential atmosphere of a stone construction in terms of light, sound reverberations, climate control, and texture. It leans on its historical background to better anchor and desacralise its contemporary formalisation. *Tiamat* is a creature in the making that transforms Gothic architecture, desert sand formations and stereotomy, to morph into a powerful organism setting new standards for contemporary architecture.

In our work, the way the stones are woven into each other is not only determined by the precision in cutting that is produced by technology and machinery, but also the unique skills of master craftsmen and a deep knowledge of the material. We use machines, not as something that can replace crafts or provide new forms, but as a new tool that is added to the set used by an artisan or craftsman. Our work is always linked to a very precise form of local knowledge that already exists; adding the machine is just an enhancement that allows us to work faster.

We are opposed to the idea of segregating design from production, which is a tendency that is shaping contemporary architecture. Advanced software and technology are only encouraging architects to build more corporate studios, where architects basically work behind screens, and after a certain number of months or years, they draft a design for a building that they then rely on other people to interpret and produce. There's no direct link. Architecture should be conceived with consideration to the urban or architectural conditions, as well as to the craft and material conditions. For us, this link is inseparable, whether we're working in architecture, furniture, or even cultural programs. Everything is born from an ongoing conversation with the makers.

All Purpose, 2021, AAU Anastas. Venice Architecture Biennale.

Elias and Yousef Anastas are partners at AAU Anastas, a Bethlehem-based architecture studio that integrates crafts with architecture at scales that vary from furniture design to territorial explorations. *Tiamat* is the latest iteration of the *Stone Matters* research project, which studies the possibilities of combining historical stone building methods with modern technologies to promote the use of structural stone in contemporary architecture. Inspired by the intrinsic geometry of desert sand dunes, *Tiamat* morphs the Gothic-inspired structural systems and pointed arches found across Palestine, Syria and Lebanon to create a vault with ribs.

Tiamat, 2024, AAU Anastas. Exhibition view, *Arab Design Now*, 2024.

Mary-Lynn and Carlo Massoud are a sibling design duo based in Lebanon. Guided by a sense of fun and trial and error, they experiment with innovative approaches to designing common objects, ranging from architectural interiors and sculptural pieces characterised by elements of colour and fantasy. *Shiitake* is one such installation, inspired by the fungi, which thrives in the most unexpected places. An ode to the interplay of reality and fantasy, the creation comprises five floor lamps of varying sizes and forms.

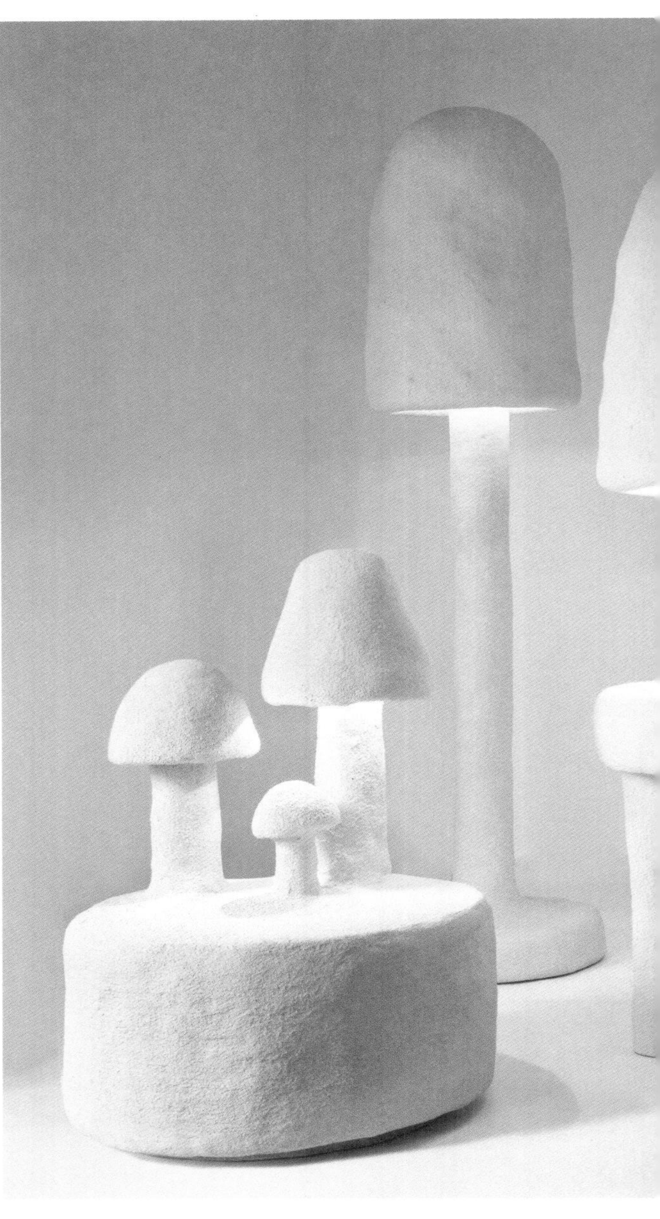

Shiitake, 2024, Mary-Lynn & Carlo.

Mary-Lynn & Carlo

Architects Independent is a Doha-based Finnish/Kuwaiti collective founded by Thomas Modeen and Maysaa Al-Mumin with an interest in engaging and designing environments and artefacts at varying scales. Their approach aims to hone the essence of each design to its cultural, social, aesthetic, or even whimsical core. Their collection of wearable artefacts, named *The Plant & Weed Rings*, is inspired by the flowers, grasses, weeds and trees of Doha, and challenges conventional notions of how jewellery is worn, perceived and valued. The designs were fabricated through the lost-wax-casting process, utilising 3D printed models.

Architects Independent

The Plant & Weed Rings, 2022–2023, Architects Independent.

"It's challenging, catalytic, enriching, collaborative, occasionally disconcerting, but ultimately electrifying to be a creative in the region today."

Thomas Modeen and Maysaa Al-Mumin

The Plant & Weed Rings, 2022–2023, Architects Independent.

Nada Rizk

Nada Rizk is a Lebanese multidisciplinary visual artist and designer based in Beirut. She works with clay, marble and other natural materials, and her designs are often inspired by nature, aiming to redefine our relationship with the environment. The two series *Neptune's Cup* and *Cliona Patera* draw inspiration from a recently rediscovered ocean sponge of the same name, once believed to be extinct. The cups are shaped to resemble the sponge's iconic goblet shape and are carved in different natural marbles. Her *Cocoon* installation is composed of unfired clay sculptures, hand-built using the coiling technique—a practice employed by potters for millennia, somewhat akin to the way larvae construct their cocoons.

Cliona Patera series, 2023, Nada Rizk.

Left: *Cocoon Installation*, 2018, Nada Rizk. Exhibition view, *Arab Design Now*, 2024. Below: Neptune's Cup series, 2018, Nada Rizk.

Christian Zahr Studio

Christian Zahr Studio is a Beirut-based practice working at the intersection of architecture, landscape design, object design, and art. His forms are an agglomeration of unpredictable and predesigned processes, archetypal and fictional, archaeological and geological. During the pandemic lockdown, Christian created the *Concrete Memories Collection*, in which he envisioned homes transformed into caves, and rooms into intimate primitive landscapes. The objects are co-created with nature; they are handmade but textured by means of dripping water.

The Concrete Memories Collection, 2021, Christian Zahr Studio.

Architect and urbanist **Fatma Al Sehlawi** comments on Qatar's rapid development, and the importance of preserving traditional craft cultures in building a national identity.

Like our neighbouring Gulf states, pre-oil Qatar was a peninsula with an economy based on coastal fishing and pearling, sea-trading towns, and nomadic inland settlements. During these humble times, people were ingenious in the ways they designed and constructed their homes. While coastal dwellers used local mud, stones, coral and palm fronds to build their intricate courtyard houses and breeze-catching alleyways, the inland desert communities depended on their sheep for wool to weave their tensile shelters, and on natural dyes to create their storytelling patterns. Regional trade brought new building materials to Qatar, such as stained glass from Iran and wooden beams from India, as well as a variety of architectural styles, including the use of pastel-coloured floral ornamentations from Pakistan, and the use of stone cladding from Lebanon. These influences were accelerated by the increase in migration to Qatar from the Levant, Southeast Asia, and East Africa, which brought in a rich palette of styles, materials, methods and trends. Till today, designs are constantly evolving in method and material.

Since the discovery of oil, Qatar has witnessed ongoing development surges. Profits from the first exports of oil in 1949 and its aftermath funded the arrival of cement in the country, allowing us to build faster and larger. Major cement-based construction companies were founded to serve the increased demand, tasked with constructing what were called the 'seeds of a nation': the first airport building, the first hospital, the first dedicated school buildings, the first radio station, and many more. This period also saw the beginning of the metamorphosis of Doha from a small town to the modern capital city we know today.

By 1971, Qatar was no longer a British Protectorate, and the government was able to fully draft its own plans for growth and development. The next two decades were focused on building a modern nation for a modern society through state-wide planning and a focus on architectural projects in Doha. This period was transformational in terms of the city's aesthetics, scale, and modernity, in general – all scripted by foreign planning firms and renowned international architects, working under the Ministry of Public Works, Ministry of Municipality, and the Private Engineering Office led by Palestinian-American planner Hisham Qaddumi. Many of the commissioned architects were in fact from the Arab world: Ahmad Cheikha from Lebanon, Kamal El Kafrawi from Egypt, Rifaat Chadirji from Iraq, to name a few, which added a regional design approach to the period. A new modern language of architecture, public art, and the public realm appeared everywhere in the country, and particularly in Doha. It was a new language, yes, but very much rooted in local architectural elements, and responsive to the local climatic conditions.

Another pinnacle moment in architecture and design took place from the mid-1990s onwards, with 'mega-projects' such as Education City, Aspire Zone, Hamad Medical City, and many more launched as part of the new vision for the country under a new leader. The Museum of Islamic Art, designed by I.M. Pei, opened in 2008, displaying a plethora of arts and crafts from the Islamic world, and instigating a ripple effect in the region for the construction of landmark cultural institutions. When the Virginia Commonwealth University School of the Arts (VCUarts) Qatar opened in 1998, it was the country's first specialised arts and design school and the first international branch university to open in Qatar Foundation's Education City. Many of our established designers and artists in Qatar are graduates of this school.

From 2010 onwards, and following Qatar's successful bid to host the FIFA World Cup 2022, the country took advantage of this new challenge to deliver major infrastructure projects such as Qatar Rail, the complete upgrade of Doha's public realm, sports facilities, and stadiums. Many new cultural institutions were also developed to cater to the increase in visitors to the country and to incubate a generation of creative talent: public artists, sculptors, architects, furniture designers, film makers, musicians, graphic designers, product designers, jewellery designers, and many more. The year 2022 was specifically dedicated to the MENASA region, within the annual Years of Culture program, illustrating the fact that the World Cup was designed to not only portray Qatar to the rest of the world, but rather to portray the whole region.

A few months prior to the FIFA World Cup, His Highness the Emir of Qatar requested the initiation of a Qatar Blueprint to create a nation-wide activation plan for the future of Qatar post-2022: to define Qatar's cultural scene and its regional and global cultural positioning after the World Cup. Here I refer to 'culture' in a broader context: as an overarching sector that covers multiple areas, geographies, ecologies, demographics, histories, traditions, crafts, industries, and so on. The focus for a long time has been on Doha, which is the main municipality of Qatar, and the Blueprint is really an exercise to expose what the other seven municipalities have to offer, and the developments needed. In most cases, it is necessary to approach this carefully and sensitively so as not to greatly alter the remaining identities and characters of those municipalities.

Clockwise from left: Doha Airport, 1960s. Image acquired by Atlas bookstore for *Making Doha* exhibition from Ali Darwishi. *US, HER, HIM,* 2022, Najla El Zein. Site-specific public installation at the Flag Plaza, Doha. Model of the Museum of Islamic Art, designed by I.M. Pei.

In the initial months of the Blueprint, we found great potential in an agri-belt mainly in the Al Khor and Al Thakhira Municipality. Overnight, a chain of private and state-owned farms that have existed for decades had become the action grounds responding to food-insecurity resulting from the Gulf political crisis in 2017 and the following pandemic. We found innovative agri-design, an environmental movement towards permaculture, soil science, the emergence of crafts and design from local materials, and so much more. The traditional crafts of Qatar are like those of other settlements in the region. Crafts were created out of necessity, evolving to attain a certain aesthetic and character specific to the country. The most well known are related to everyday objects such as pottery, leather tanning, wooden joinery, blacksmithing, *sadu* weaving, ornamental gypsum, and dhow building. Certain families carry a family name that indicates their original profession in a specific craft, such as Al Sayegh, known for jewellery making, Al Naddaf known for wool crafts, and Al Najjar known for joinery crafts, to name a few.

The surveys of the Qatar Blueprint have helped me identify the crafts that continue to exist as a living heritage, which serve a need rather than recalling a tradition that is practised as a performative display. One such craft is dhow building. Qatar, like Kuwait, Bahrain, and the UAE, was known as a centre for constructing dhows in the region, producing specific typologies of vessels, including those that played major roles in either trade or the protection of the region. Today, two major dhow workshops exist in Qatar, one in Doha and one in Al Ruwais. They are both operated under one entity, the Private Engineering Office, which plays a role in preserving the traditional crafts of Qatar. Descendants of dhow builders oversee the work carried out by craftsmen mainly from India. The same techniques are used, and the same materials, such as wooden beams from West India, are imported, yet at a more controlled quality and higher measures of safety. There is still a need for more to be done to employ this craftsmanship and know-how in experimenting with its possibilities and producing other objects that may benefit from such a skill.

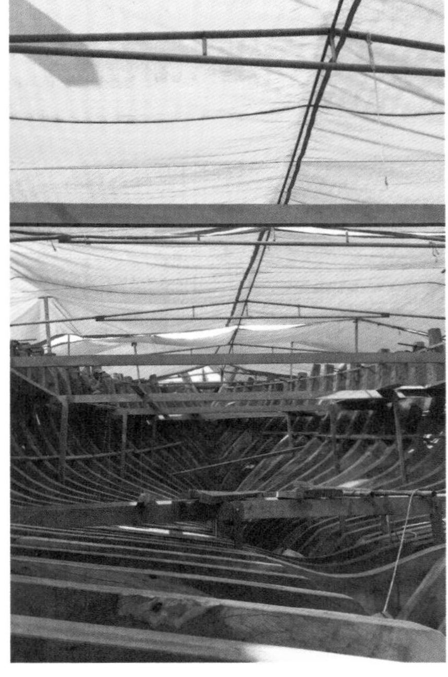

In the course of the surveys, we came to realise that many of the traditional crafts of Qatar have been reduced to performative displays that one can see and experience in the old Souq Waqif and other cultural centres. Or in some cases, the artefacts are produced in the traditional way but are made elsewhere in the region and imported to this country. We have attempted to locate people and places where the crafts are still practised genuinely and have identified many women who still have knowledge of *sadu* weaving, for example, a craft passed down between generations of women to provide the textile needed for tent shelters and interior furnishings for tents and houses alike. In the past, each *sadu* design held a meaning behind its specific patterns and reflected what natural dyes and fibres were available; the National Museum of Qatar documents this craft in great detail in one of its galleries. Different designers

have also collaborated with the women *sadu* weavers to create new pieces based on the traditional techniques. One example is Asma Derouiche, who has worked with *sadu* weavers, and traditional leather tanners, as well as other craftspeople based at Souq Waqif, with the intention of bringing such crafts into contemporary practice. The initiatives of Heenat Salma also come to mind, an ecological farm in Qatar, which collaborates with craftsmen/women to utilise the natural materials the farm produces, offering workshops and residencies for vocational training and masterclasses. They've supported *sadu* weavers and brought them to the public eye through exhibits, and also supported designers such as Abdulrahman Al Muftah through a residency that focused on Qatari clay and its potentials.

As for my practice as an architect, in 2017 Nasser Al Amadi and I founded Studio Imara to explore the possibilities of design in our geography and climate, and to look at the industry and what it allows for. We chose to focus only on local projects to expand our knowledge of working on and for this land. We also chose simplicity and minimalism in a way that celebrates the Qatari culture and environment. In the case of landscape design, we always propose local landscape typologies, native and naturalised plant palettes, and programs that include informal activities that have always been part of our heritage and relationship with the outdoors, particularly in the wilderness of the desert. Most clients are not used to such proposals, but the ideas excite them. Sometimes they feel nostalgic and at other times they see that this could be the beginning of a larger effort to develop locally with simplicity and in a way that rejects the tendency to design a place so that it looks like it is in a different country. This has been the norm within the design, architecture, and landscape fields in Qatar and, of course, in the region generally: clients wanting a park that looks like the gardens of Versailles, or a house that looks like a palace in Marrakesh, or a shopping mall that looks like a fake setting in Las Vegas. It is slow, but there is

Clockwise from left: Dhow building at the Traditional Dhow Workshop in Doha. Sadu weaving, a craft passed down through generations of Qatari women. One of the last remaining wool and cotton spinners at Souq Al Najada in Doha, known as Al Naddaf.

a great openness to abandoning this trait and luckily the major state-developers, whether for university buildings, museums, and urban expansion, are championing the movement away from imitating the foreign.

In 2019 I co-curated an exhibition, titled *Making Doha*, with Rem Koolhaas and Samir Bantal to coincide with the opening of the National Museum of Qatar. It told the story of Doha's development, from the arrival of cement to today and its ongoing drive towards delivering the Qatar National Vision in the year 2030. The exhibition was wrapped by a 115-metre-long curtain printed with archival images, and featured 70 years of photos, architectural models, plans, texts, films, and oral histories documenting the cultural and construction milestones in the nation's unique journey towards modernisation.

The research engine behind the exhibition started at Atlas Bookstore, a store I cofounded in 2015 with my sister Reem, who shares my passion for the architecture and urbanism of West Asia and North Africa. For its first four years, Atlas was located at the Doha Sheraton Hotel, which is itself a modernist architectural gem from 1982, designed by American architect William Pereira. The bookstore sells and displays books and magazines and acts as a reference library, with a growing collection of rare, old and out-of-print publications. Selections of our books have travelled to different exhibitions in places such as Kuwait, Bahrain, Dubai Design Days, the Vitra Design Museum, and VCUarts Qatar. Reem is now developing the collection to include environmental histories and futures of the region. An upcoming contribution by Atlas will be published in a book titled *Doha Modern*, which documents a playground project by the artist Shezad Dawood, commissioned by Qatar Museums.

Fatma Al Sehlawi

With Blueprint Qatar, we're continuing the in-depth surveys and will soon follow with design and planning to build a municipality-focused, and state-wide scope to activate the full cultural potential of the country. Working on this, I see the benefits of getting everyone more engaged with other regions in Qatar. There's so

Left: Al Shaqab Village under construction, designed by Studio Imara. Above: Architectural model of an unrealised design by Arata Isozaki for the National Library of Qatar, displayed at the *Making Doha* exhibition, National Museum of Qatar, 2019.

much to explore and experience, and so much to work with, whether you're an environmentalist, a historian, an artist, a designer, or a maker. Design weeks and biennales like Design Doha are important moments in time where dense programming, exchange, and exposure to local, regional, and international design can come together to enrich the creative scene of Qatar. It is an activation of many places in the country through design displays, allowing the industry to engage with the local community. I've seen similar yet not identical programs, such as Amman Design Week, and what it brought to Jordan, in terms of visitors seeking to learn more about the local design industry and beyond. These moments are truly activators of the creative scene in their host nation.

Book display for Atlas Bookstore's reading space at Dubai Design Days. Shelving made at Al Jaddaf's dhow workshops.

Fatma Al Sehlawi is an architect and urbanist based in Doha, Qatar. She is the cofounder of Atlas Bookstore, which specialises in titles relevant to architecture and the urban environment of the Middle East and North Africa region. An experienced curator, she co-curated *Mudun: Urban Cultures in Transit* in 2017 at the Vitra Design Museum and collaborated with Rem Koolhaas and Samir Bantal of AMO on the exhibition *Making Doha* in 2019 at the National Museum of Qatar.

CHARTER OF DUBAI
Dubai - Dynamics of Bingo Urbanism
THE DUBAI HANDBOOK
The Arab City
Castles in the Sand
DUBAI VILLAS

House Between a Jujube Tree and a Palm Tree, 2024, Civil Architecture. Exhibition view, *Arab Design Now*, 2014.

Civil Architecture is a practice preoccupied with the making of buildings and the books about them. Their work asks what it means to produce architecture in a decidedly un-civil time, presenting a new civic character for a global condition. The installation *House Between a Jujube Tree and a Palm Tree* recreates an unrealised architectural proposal for a garden *majlis* or family guesthouse in Manama, Bahrain. The abstracted 1:1 model is an exploration of the symbiotic but blurred relationship between the indoor and outdoor and the family's relationship to the garden they maintain. The form of the roof responds to the process of maintaining two trees sited in the garden.

•

Civil Architecture

“To create in the Gulf is to spend a short time designing something, and a long time watching it live.”

Hamed Bukhamseen and Ali Ismail Karimi

House Between a Jujube Tree and a Palm Tree, 2024 (detail), Civil Architecture.

Desert Cast Collective was founded by Kuwait-based designers Jassim AlNashmi and Kawther Alsaffar. In their sand-cast aluminium pieces, nick-named *Zigzag*, *Puppy* and *Snake*, they present a critical alternative to the kitsch architectural motifs that have permeated Kuwait's buildings. Through these works, the designers analyse and criticise the replication of classical architectural motifs that contribute to Kuwait's struggle to develop a context-based urban identity. By re-applying borrowed regional elements and hybridised motifs from Kuwait, the works suggest an alternative practical scenario of how the phenomenon of identity could continue to evolve.

Desert Cast Collective

Towards an Identity, 2023, Desert Cast Collective.

Mohammad Sharaf is a Kuwait-based multidisciplinary artist and graphic designer, whose work focuses on social and political commentary. His installation, composed of 'bookblocks' represents a form of contemporary archaeology. Titled *After the End*, the work consists of books that contain photographs of abandoned places in Kuwait, going back 50 years. Many of these places and objects, along with their stories and history, no longer exist, while others are disappearing due to neglect or gentrification.

Mohammad Sharaf

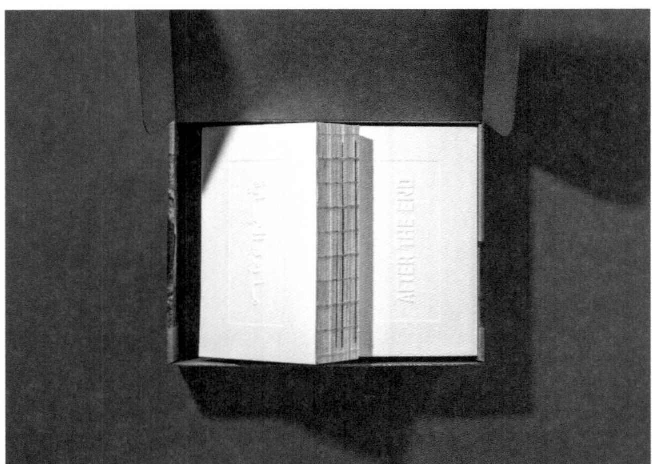

After the End, 2024, Mohammad Sharaf. Exhibition view, *Arab Design Now*, 2024.

Maryam Al-Homaid is an interdisciplinary artist and academic. Her textile works act as a record documenting the status of the continuously changing Qatari landscape, whether urban or cultural. *El Bebat* (The Construction Pipes) and *El Hawajez* (The Construction Barriers) are handmade and hand-dyed textiles that reflect on the ambitious construction boom taking place in Qatar, depicting common construction elements that have become synonymous with the country's visual identity.

Left: *El Hawajez* (The Construction Barriers), 2023, Maryam Al-Homaid.
Below: *El Bebat* (The Construction Pipes), 2023, Maryam Al-Homaid.

Maryam Al-Homaid

El Bebat (The Construction Pipes), 2023, Maryam Al-Homaid.

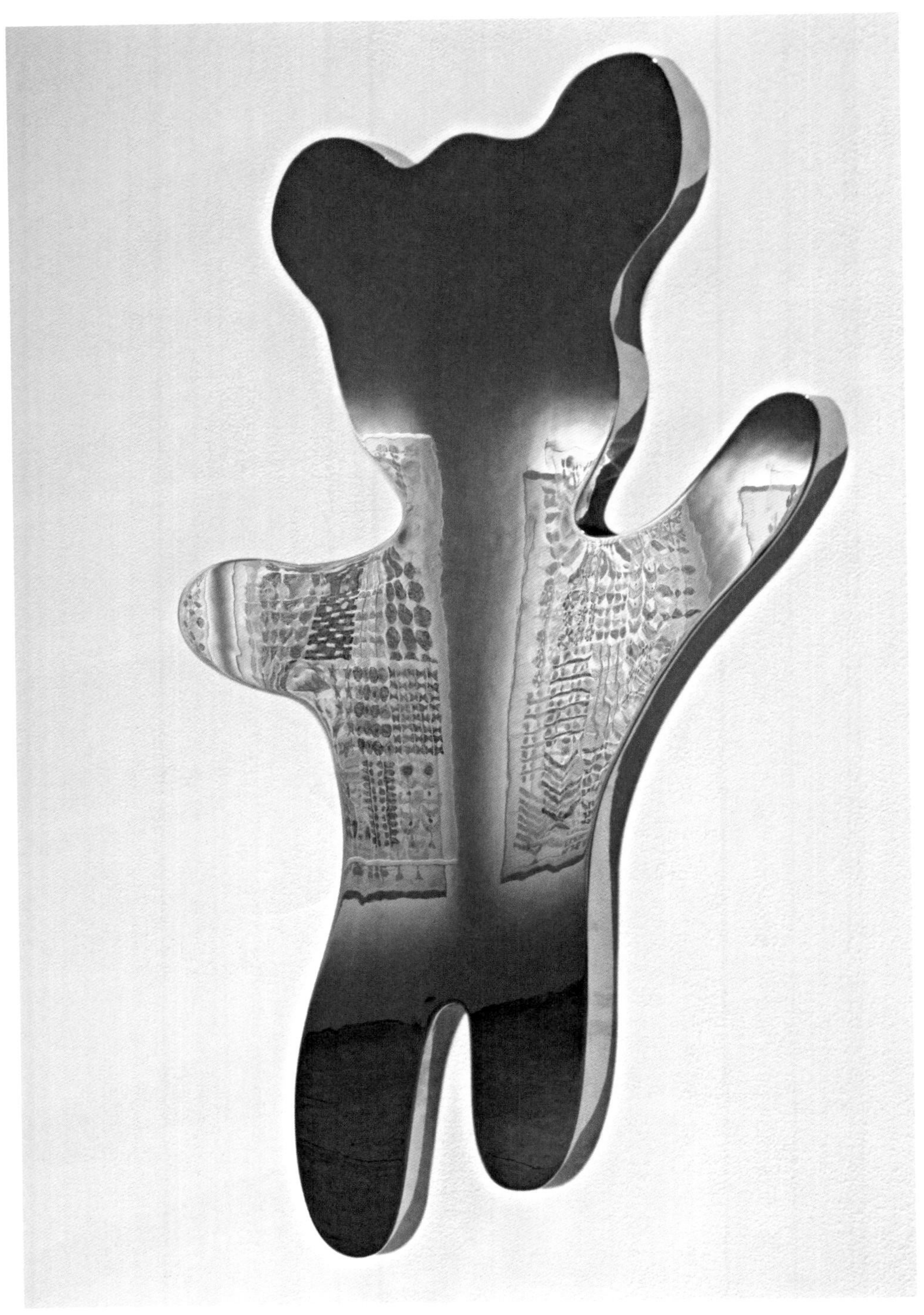

Aisha Nasser Al Sowaidi

Aisha Nasser Al Sowaidi is a Doha-based multi-disciplinary designer. Her research and design practice explores themes of home, nostalgia, childhood, memory and heritage in the context of Doha's rapid growth. *Bear with Me* is one such piece. In her own words: "*Bear with Me* is a promising mirror that looks into the future of Doha and where it's heading with all the development and construction, making it a 'future city' in progress. New cities are appearing, bridges are blooming, and streets are diverging. *Bear with Me* is a reassuring phrase, suggesting that time adds value, making a new place in future memory for us and for generations to come."

Bear with Me, 2021, Aisha Nasser Al Sowaidi. Exhibition view, Arab Design Now, 2024.

As an architect and designer, **Dima Srouji**'s research-based practice has guided her thinking about archaeology and glassblowing, and how preserving the craft, interacting with it, and transforming it becomes an act of resistance.

✦

My faith in Palestine comes from my attachment to the layers of the land, my home. One of the dimensions I'm most drawn to is the extension of the land itself, and its transformation into different artefacts. Materials that are used to make objects, like mud, sand and glass, resonate deeply with me.

I came across glass blowing by accident. When I returned home after my studies abroad, I was working with Riwaq[1] on a renovation project in the historic village of Jaba'. That's where I met Marwan and Abu Marwan Twam, a family of glassblowers who were making chemistry sets for a lab from glass tubes. It was addictive witnessing the glass in its alchemical state. There is something truly magical about the process. The forms being created were as contemporary as the objects I made when I was in graduate school, studying with Greg Lynn, who was very influential in my work. Greg's nickname in the architecture world is the 'Blob Guy' because of his experimentation with architectural forms, using advanced computer software really early on.

I was interested in continuing this experimentation, so I started working with the Twam family, designing with 3D modelling software and making strange objects. They thought I was crazy at first, but now we learn things together. I bring my laptop to the shop and show them drawings and sometimes they'll give advice and tell me you need to make this shorter or longer for it to sit right. Sometimes we experiment with new techniques like melting the glass and pouring it into metal to see what happens. That's how we learn from each other and how the design process works. In this space, the glass project *Hollow Forms* was born.

Working with the Twam family is a beautiful experience. They are a treasure in our history of craft. Their shop is in their home, and there are three generations working there simultaneously. The matriarch Im Marwan comes in with coffee and tea, and prepares large meals for the guests as if they were part of the family. Palestinian hospitality becomes an element in the process of collaboration and making. I have certainly learned more from them than they have from me. They obviously have years of experience, and sometimes I worry that I get more out of the collaboration than they do. Ethically, I find it imperative

1. Riwaq: a centre for the preservation of architectural heritage in Palestine.

to highlight makers rather than to think of them as anonymous fabricators. Designers tend to use the excuse that the craftspeople would prefer anonymity, which I find to be absurd. Either the makers are not happy with the collaboration and would prefer not to be named, or there is not enough support coming from the designer regarding the credit they deserve. I don't, however, mean to understate the role of the design in the process, as I deeply believe design is critical in making sure the craft survives and thrives to be sustained by future generations.

There is a vast history of glass blowing in the region, with a significant social, cultural and economic impact. Many people think it originated in Rome and Venice, but that's not true. The history of glassblowing begins in Palestine, and it has been a living craft for centuries. The first people in the world to blow glass were in the south of Acre, where there is a small river called Nahr Naamain containing high levels of silica in the sand. The raw material that was extracted from our rivers to produce glass was being exported to glass blowing centres in Cairo and Sidon as early as the Roman period. It was an industrialised system with massive manufacturers of glass, and over time visitors brought the practice back with them to the rest of Europe.

Craft is an organism that is constantly being shaped by internal and external information. It cannot be understood as static or exclusive to a particular location. As people moved across borders over the years, craftsmen were trained by experts from multiple parts of our region. In the past we had Turkish and Egyptian craftsmen training Palestinians how to create plaster carving for the windows of al Aqsa. The mother of pearl inlays in Bethlehem now continue to be produced in South America as Christian Palestinians migrated there at the turn of the century. Historically, there was a constant knowledge exchange that is still ongoing today.

Nonetheless, there are always some differences and formal signifiers that can help identify a specific vessel's provenance, where it was blown, and by whose hands and breath. This is still the case everywhere. You can tell which pieces were blown by the Twam family in Jaba' who use lampworking techniques, which is a more contemporary practice, as opposed to the glassblowers in Hebron, who are more identified with traditional methods. But even within the same

Above: *Alienation*, 2017, Dima Srouji.
Below: *Almost Roman*, 2020, Dima Srouji.

technique of making, different family members work with the material differently and their marks are printed on each vessel. Each craftsperson is unique, and they have an impact on the larger identity of the national craft, which is constantly moving and growing, taking multiple shapes over the years. Glass makers in Hebron now recycle old glass bottles or buy recycled glass from glass factories in the city to be melted again in their furnaces. Traditionally sand was used to make raw glass, but this is no longer sustainable. Today, the Twam family works with borosilicate glass for its durability, using the lampworking techniques.

Palestine has a rich history of craft: embroidery, olive wood carving, straw weaving, ceramics, carpet weaving, copperwork, mother of pearl carving, and so on. Archaeological surveys offer the best evidence we have of the pivotal role of craft in the history of the region. There are reconstruction drawings done for different archaeological reports that reimagine how glass furnaces were built with mudbrick to melt sand. Tiny glass fragments can still be found on the sites where archaeological artefacts were removed. The tiny shards are treasured by antiquities dealers in Jerusalem or Bethlehem, who work with local jewellers to turn them into beautiful rings and necklaces. If you were to go to the old cities, you could buy a piece of archaeological evidence of the ancient glass blowing industry! I'm still learning about the material history; there's a lot to it and it's hard to trace all the way back. There's power in using the objects or vessels themselves as a way of telling the story of what it means for archaeological artefacts to be displaced.

The archaeological surveys that were done in Palestine are a source of inspiration in my design process, with drawings of fragments and vessels functioning as the early sketches for some of my collections. Inspiration from the relationship between design and archaeology began with my early interest in the work of Giovanni Battista Piranesi (1720–1758). He was one of the first people to ever map the city of Rome, but he drew it in a way where he was taking archaeological monuments and scaling them up and scaling them down and placing them in completely different locations. It was a political statement that time and space are not linear. He also included his own imagined monuments in his mapping of the city. That's really interesting to think about, as an architect, because archaeologists are normally so married to the idea of linear history. I always channel Piranesi in my *Hollow Forms* work as well as in my larger practice, which is much more concerned with the ground in the same way Piranesi was.

Abu Marwan blowing a vessel in the workshop in Jaba', Palestine.

As an architect, I came from the understanding of archaeology as a physical space, or an exploration of the ground as an excavated space. Archaeology helps us think about who we are as human beings but it is also a vulnerable practice and can be weaponised by those who want to produce subjective work. Archaeologists have the right to determine what's valuable and what's not and are often not interested in a complex and multilayered narrative, preferring rather a singular and straightforward one that serves their interests.

In my case, I'm really trying to bring awareness to the industry of glass blowing because it's dying. The preservation of craft and culture is the most important work required to maintain momentum towards liberation. I think our role in this case is not to be paralysed by nostalgia. We can respect our traditions and champion them through joy and experimentation without fearing external influences. Today, there are no glassblowers left in Jordan, and in Palestine there's only the Natsheh family in Hebron and the Twam family in Jaba', who I'm working with. Syria was the most important place for glass blowing but after the war that is no longer the case, and in Lebanon, I think there's only one left, with the same in Egypt.

Then there's the question of the architectural scale of glass. The history of glass in architecture is very understudied. People really only consider it through the lens of the Crystal Palace or Bruno Taut's pavilion. There is a lot of potential in exploring this further through larger installations that could incorporate other crafts as well. Traditionally glass was used for partitions, walls, floor tiles, doors and windows, in conjunction with mother of pearl, stone and plaster. I started this experimentation at the first Islamic Art Biennial in Jeddah with the installation titled *Maintaining the Sacred*, which looks at the history of the Dome of the Rock windows that have been destroyed repeatedly by the Israeli Occupation Forces.

I'm also really interested in transparency as a concept and its relationship to stage and theatre design and have been inspired by Bob Wilson's work recently. There is something about making objects as props that allows us to tell stories differently, which I love. Imagine a play where there were no people, only things telling stories. There's an ontological discussion here regarding the idea of human-to-human relationships, which are considered as superior to object-to-human relationships. A lot of

Ghosts, 2019, Dima Srouji. Amman Design Week / Coming Museum of Glass.

contemporary philosophers will tell you that human-to-human relationships are more critical that from an anti-capitalist point of view, all value should be thought of in terms of human value rather than object value. But for me it totally depends on how you define objects, not as commodities or in relation to monetary value, but rather in terms of cultural and spiritual value or memory.

I've lived in around ten cities in the last ten years. Every time I move, I bring objects with me that make me feel at home, whether it's books or plants or a rug. It's a projection of my memory and emotions onto these things. There is this layer that you impose onto the surface of an object or on to its identity that makes it more valuable for you. I like to believe that there is something intrinsic in an object – not that it has a spirit, but that imprinting memory onto its membranes actually somehow changes its physical structure and its value in reality. There is this connection between the human and object after some kind of interaction. This is where fiction gets exciting. Value is constantly changing. An object within the context of a glass vitrine is valued differently from an identical object placed on my grandmother's shelf at home. One might be financially more valuable than the other, whereas the other could be emotionally or socially more valuable. The distinction between collective and individual value is also an interesting point. A blanket from my childhood could be worth a lot more to me than it would to a stranger on the street, but yet that stranger may also have a memory of a childhood blanket of theirs that is relatable. There is an interesting moment there when value can be shared and transmitted between the collective, because we all have some shared experience on a basic level.

Artefacts are objects that are historic in their nature and clearly embody multiple layers within them. They carry stories of a larger stretch of time, both past and future, than some everyday things. A museum object is different in that it belongs to an institution in some sense. I don't think of my pieces as museum objects but I do think of them as artefacts that are somehow projections of multiple places and times into inanimate form, which carries a weight that archaeological artefacts might contain. You could think of this as a process of mimicking and transmitting meaning through making. I think humans can perceive characteristics and qualities of certain objects – if they listen carefully.

Transparent Histories, 2024, Dima Srouji. Exhibition view, *Arab Design Now*, 2024.

Dima Srouji is a Palestinian architect and visual artist who works with glass, text, archives, maps, plaster casts and film. Understanding each medium as an evocative object and emotional companion helps her question the meaning of cultural heritage and public space in the larger context of the Middle East, and of Palestine in particular. Her piece *Transparent Histories* dives into the forgotten history of glass in architecture. Inspired by Piranesi's drawings, the panel depicts a map of architectural monuments, both real and fictionalised, in Jerusalem, a city convoluted in its strata, with layers of hidden narratives waiting to be excavated. The monuments are engraved and carved into a stone surface embedded with honey-coloured glass pieces.

Sahel Alhiyari is an architect and artist leading an interdisciplinary design practice in Amman, with a diverse portfolio spanning architecture, urban design, interiors, exhibition design, and installations. *Eleven* is composed of 11 fluted columns, erected from vertically stacked hand-crafted terracotta segments. Conjuring orders of classical antiquity, yet underscoring the vitality of contemporary materiality and technique, the columns rely on moulding and forming rather than the cutting and carving used in ancient architecture. The craftsmanship, with its adobe-like malleability, recalls techniques used to make pottery, and showcases texture and imperfection as integral outcomes.

Eleven, 2024. Sahel Alhiyari. Exhibition view, *Arab Design Now*, 2024.

• Sahel Alhiyari

Amine Asselman

Amine Asselman is a Moroccan visual artist, designer and educator based in Tetouan, Morocco. His work *Metamorphosis* is a geometric research project that arises from his doctoral thesis on Tetouan Zellige, a unique artisanal technique in Morocco, which has been classified by UNESCO as threatened to disappear. In his thesis, Amine generates new geometric languages based on arithmetic permutations and Zellige patterns, creating a dialogue between heritage and the contemporary. The hand-cut ceramic tesserae, glazed with mineral oxides and assembled with resin, create a body with an organic quality despite the composition being entirely based on arithmetic permutations.

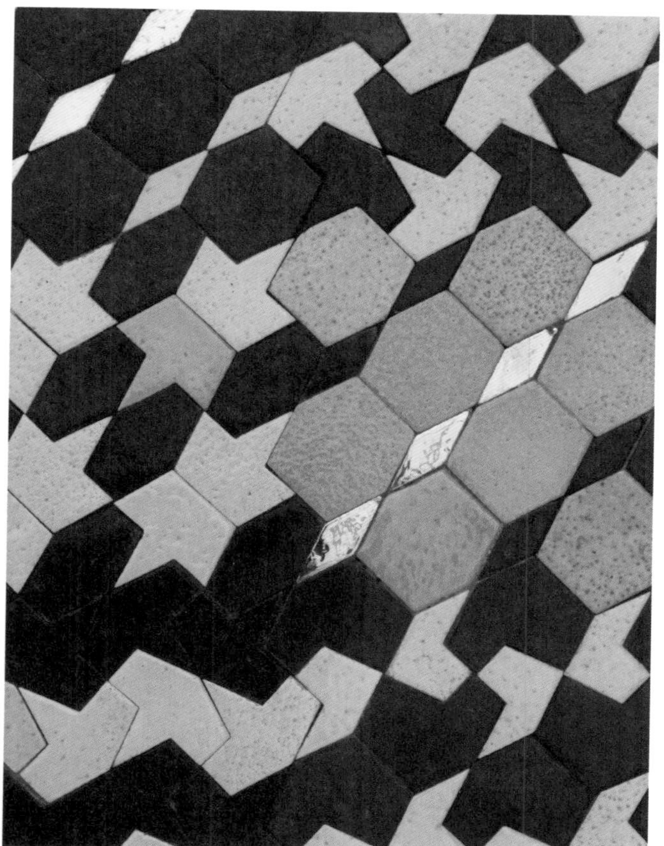

Metamorphosis, 2024, Amine Asselman.

Hamza Kadiri for Ateliers Courbet

Hamza Kadiri is a Moroccan artist hailing from a long lineage of experts in wood working. He honed his artistry during his apprenticeships in Japan, and from his Casablanca workshop, where he uses vintage machines and tools. *Sculptural Console AM7V1-3*, which is entirely hand-carved by Kadiri, was created using a process that unites two opposite forces, one seemingly destructive, the other restorative. The wood is first exposed to sudden bursts of flame, then brushed smooth as it cools. Inspired by mythology and classical art, his second work *Bench 01* is made using the traditional Japanese *Shou Sugi Ban* technique, a process by which wood is cut into planks, dried in open air, burned on the surface to create a thin layer of char, then brushed and sealed. Hamza is represented by Ateliers Courbet in New York City.

Sculptural Console AM7V1-3, 2023, Hamza Kadiri for Ateliers Courbet.

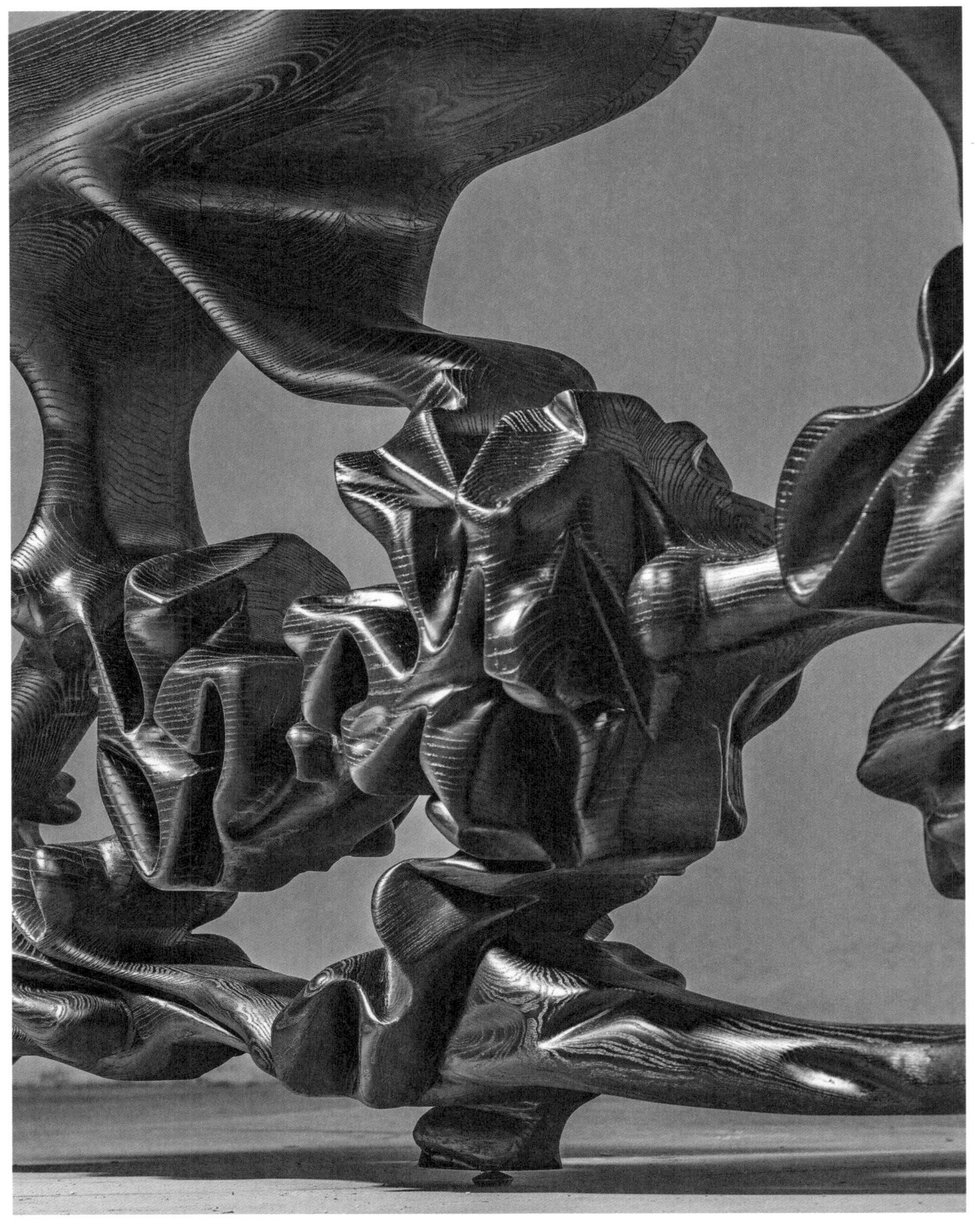

"I use vintage machines and tools from Morocco–it's moving to see the marks left behind by the artisans who once used them. I enjoy prolonging their lifespan, incorporating them into contemporary creation. Their soul and energy nourish my atelier. I cannot imagine creating in a high-tech studio."

Hamza Kadiri

Sculptural Console AM7V1-3, 2023, Hamza Kadiri for Ateliers Courbet.

bahraini-danish is an architecture and design studio based in Bahrain and Denmark, and founded by Batool Al Shaikh, Maitham Almubarak, and Christian Vennerstrøm Jensen. The studio highlights their cultural differences, both socially and professionally, as a means of creation. Their installation *A Bench That Interlocks and Interweaves* is composed of identical units, which link together in a chain. The individual elements are rigid but have flexible joints that allow the bench to expand, contract and bend. The bent metal tubes convey stability and strength even as they lean on each other for support.

A Bench That Interlocks and Interweaves, 2024, bahraini-danish. Exhibition view, *Arab Design Now*, 2024.

bahraini-danish

Najla El Zein is a Beirut-born designer currently living and working in Amsterdam. She experiments with the scale, mass, void and materiality of objects and their relation to their surroundings. Her latest stone bench, named *Lover's Bench*, is hand sculpted in Ceppo, a unique stone that is geologically formed from compressed marble fragments. The bench is composed of two elements that fit into one another and interlock. Also centred around the notion of interactions, Najla's new sculpture series *Ensemble* experiments with glass in an approach born out of synchronised individual and collaborative human gestures, which include pressing, pushing, twisting, pulling, curling and folding.

Najla El Zein

Lovers Bench, 2023, Najla El Zein.

Lovers Bench (detail), 2023, Najla El Zein.

Ensemble, 01-03, 2023, Najla El Zein.

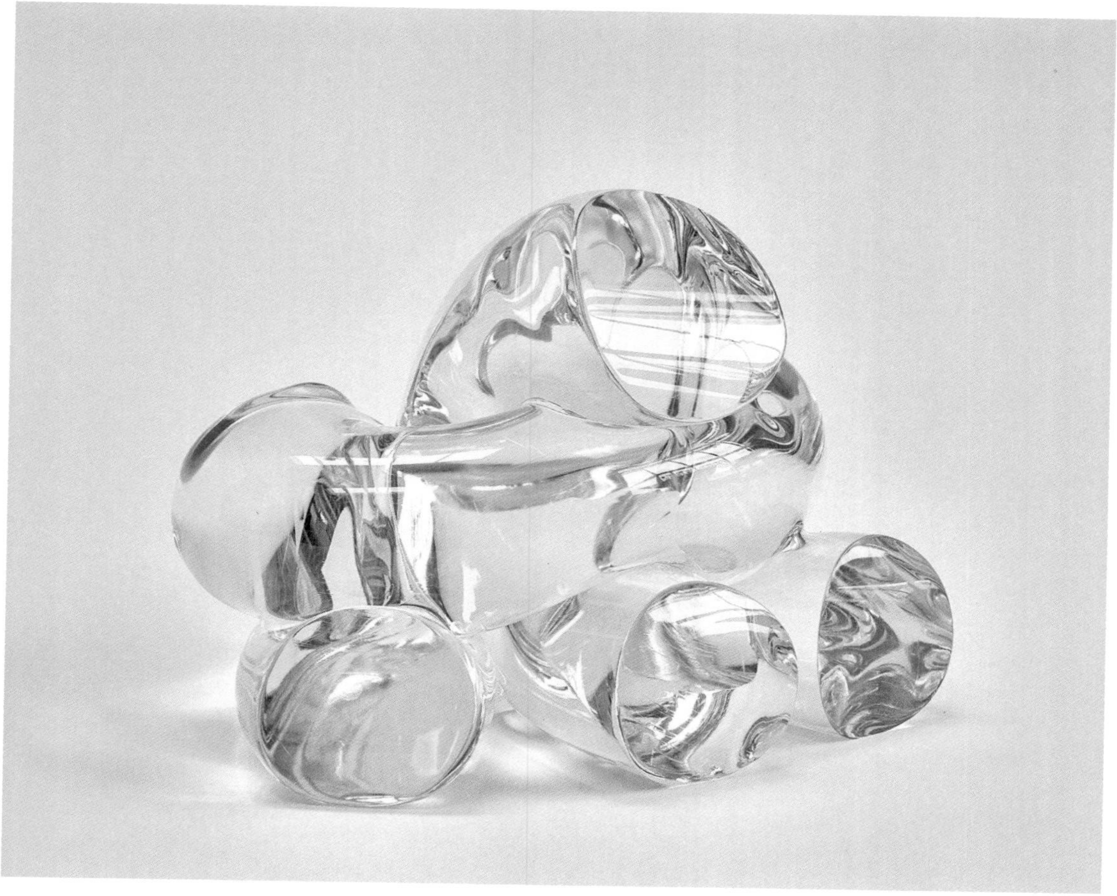

Naqsh Collective search deep within their Palestinian origins into *tatreez*, a traditional folk craft that is rich, unique, and steeped in meaning, but also under threat of erasure. Beyond being a mere act of preservation of tradition and identity, their work situates the craft as an active, living and evolving practice – one that uses modern materials, tools and aesthetics.

✦

When we first started Naqsh, we knew we wanted to work on products that reflect us personally – two women, born and raised in Amman, inheritors of this region's rich visual culture of geometries, calligraphy, and Islamic patterns, while also craving a modern and contemporary aesthetic.

During the Arab Spring, there was a revolutionary spirit all around, and it led us to reflect on our identities and heritage. We are originally Palestinian. Our grandparents escaped Palestine during the Nakba (the catastrophe of 1948) and came to Amman as refugees. There is a strong emotion and narrative surrounding this critical moment in history and the resulting lifestyle, which is so closely tied to Palestine, although it is a land we are now prohibited from returning to or living in. This is a dissonance we inherited.

Growing up, our mother and grandmother taught us *tatreez* (embroidery) based on a simple need or household chore; to create tablecloths, pillows and thobes (traditional dresses). It was a routine social activity, where embroidering a thobe would sometimes become an all consuming collaborative family project.

Later, after training as an architect, I started to see the patterns of *tatreez* as a series of AutoCAD lines. My sister Nermeen and I would draw a few elements and start experimenting with the forms, stretching some lines, but keeping the embroidery at the heart of it. This was a eureka moment for us; at once very familiar and also exciting.

In the beginning, we decided to work with only 12 patterns on which we would base our intervention and engage in experiments of deconstruction and reconstruction to introduce a new architectural language to them. Sometimes when you look at our work, you don't really see the cross-stitch, you see geometric patterns and shapes and extrusions. The trained eye will be able to trace it back to the traditional patterns. No matter how much we work outside the box when it comes to *tatreez*, and no matter how much we move away from the needle and thread, you can still recognise the pattern, which is our own way of preserving them. *Tatreez* belongs to a collective group of creative Palestinian women. It is a collective art. So we didn't feel we could just take it and add or remove without justification.

Our discovery of Widad Kawar and Tiraz[1] in Jordan was a very formative experience for us at Naqsh – it was almost a divine union when we came together. Widad is an expert in *tatreez* and has a wealth of stories to share about each dress in her collection, which she painstakingly collected and preserved over many years. In fact, in 2013 she invited us to do our first show, which was a real honour for us. To have this approval from someone with that level of experience, and to see the open and welcoming reaction of someone from her generation to the new interventions and ideas we introduced, was an indication of how progressive she was. She embraced our work without fear. She could see that in our own way, we were invested in not only preserving, but also practising *tatreez* as well.

We didn't intend for embroidery to become such a big part of our work, but when we saw the reaction of the audience, we knew we had hit a powerful note. People to this day will send us images of their grandmothers' or their mothers' dresses, pictures of their homes in Palestine, documents and other memorabilia, each sharing their story with us, and clearly still holding on to them with deep sentimentality. It's no longer just about creating design elements, it's about connecting with people. That's our treasure.

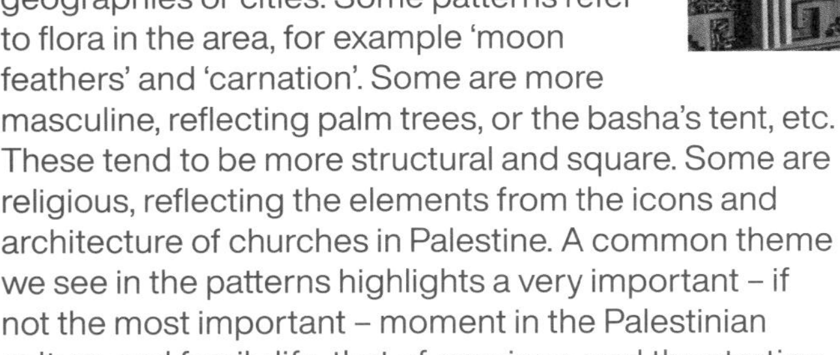

Below: *Sadu Walnut*, 2018 (detail), Naqsh Collective. Right: *Bridal Rug*, 2017, Naqsh Collective. Exhibition view, Thrust for Solidarity, Tiraz, 2017.

Tatreez is a powerful tool for storytelling and is a language in its own right. It can reveal layers about society, beyond being just a beautiful craft. Certain stitches and patterns are associated with certain geographies or cities. Some patterns refer to flora in the area, for example 'moon feathers' and 'carnation'. Some are more masculine, reflecting palm trees, or the basha's tent, etc. These tend to be more structural and square. Some are religious, reflecting the elements from the icons and architecture of churches in Palestine. A common theme we see in the patterns highlights a very important – if not the most important – moment in the Palestinian culture and family life, that of marriage, and the starting of a new family, or the fusing of two families. There is a

1. Tiraz: Widad Kawar Home for Arab Dress is a museum and centre in Amman, Jordan, which holds the most complete collection of Palestinian, Jordanian and other Arab costumes from the 19th and 20th centuries, with over 2000 costumes and weavings.

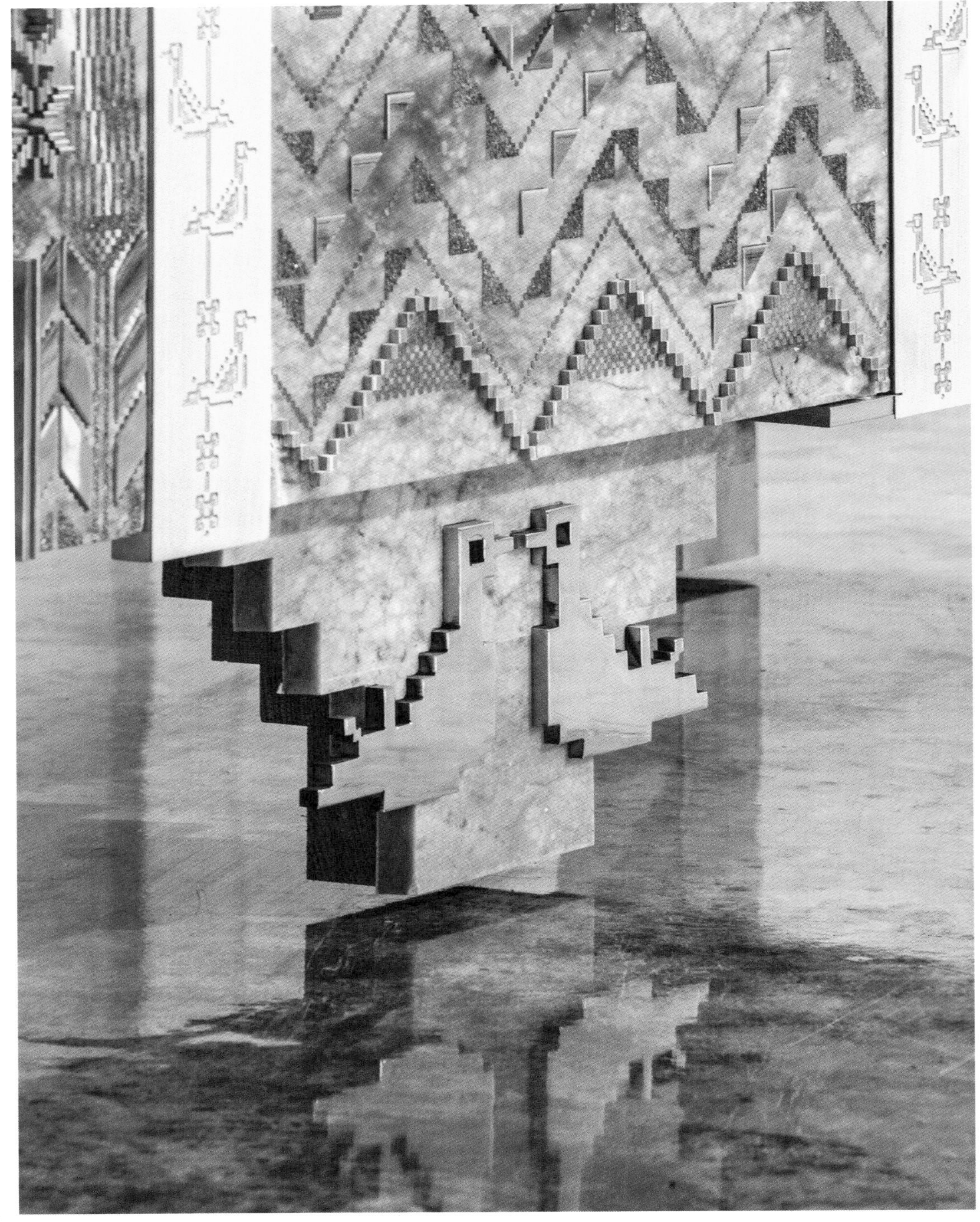

practice in our culture where the family will prepare a *jhaz* (trousseau) for the bride as she prepares herself to move to a new house. Sometimes, families start preparing for the bride and her marriage from the day she is born, and it may take years and sometimes travel to other cities to get it all ready.

One of the motifs related to marriage is a specific stitch depicting the relationship of a bride with her mother in law – it looks like two birds going head to head with one another. In true comedic fashion, they didn't mind acknowledging the tensions that often occur in that important relationship.

We wanted to reflect these practices in our pieces. When our sister Shireen had a daughter, we created a project called *Jhazek ya Shams*, named after our niece and dedicated to her. It was a moment where we all came together and created a line of products for Shams as a new woman in our family. At Naqsh, we are three sisters – Nisreen, the architect, Nermeen, the graphic designer, and our third sister Shireen, who is also a partner and manages our affairs. So the whole family mobilised, using patterns from embroidery to celebrate the newborn girl and as a celebration of this strong maternal lineage. We created a line of products – a tray, a piece inspired by a bride's pillow, a chest of drawers, etc.

The bride's thobe is also a reflection of social status – those who are wealthy can sometimes use gold threads. There is a stitch that records the size of a home – one floor, two floors, three floors – and as their homes got bigger, the women would show this change in their thobes, making the dress a dynamic canvas on which the artwork evolves as their social status changes.

When a woman became a widow, she was expected to take apart all of the embroidery on her dress, unthreading it stitch by stitch, thread by thread, removing all colour from it. If she wanted to embroider a new one, it would be monochrome – a black thobe with indigo dyed threads. The idea of disposable fashion was not present. If for example, a woman gained weight, she wouldn't throw out the old dress and make a new one, but add fabric to it and make it larger, with new embroidery on it. So the dress grows with her as well.

Through our research, we once came across an embroidery pattern called 'Sofa'. At the time, we laughed, and thought, why would they create a specific stitch

Green Bridal Chest, 2023 (detail), Naqsh Collective.

for a sofa? Then we were commissioned by the Jordan National Gallery of Fine Arts to create a chair for an exhibition called *Chair with a Tale*. So we took our usual trip to Tiraz to visit Aunty Widad for information. She told us about the 'sofa' stitch and its companion 'orange' stitch and how they reflect the story of Jaffa and its people. Jaffa was historically a highly developed wealthy city with a trade port and bustling commercial centre exporting the famous Jaffa oranges around the world. This meant that its people were some of the first to bring in expensive goods from abroad – and one of those goods was a specific style of Italian sofa. This intertwined legacy of the oranges that paid for the sofas was used as a basis for the chair we designed for this commission.

Jaffa of course is very personal to us because of our family origins, and it is from that city that our family was expelled. So naturally, it takes the lion's share of our focus, although we have only ever been to Jaffa for a few lucky hours. We understood that a large part of the cultural wealth of Palestine was centred there. It's amazing to see how *tatreez*, although it was mostly a folk craft practised by the farmers in rural areas, was celebrated nonetheless by modern urban dwellers, despite having access to the latest fashion from around the world. It was an honest and pure form of cultural expression and identity.

The route between Damascus, Jaffa, and Cairo was a central nervous system where a lot of cultural and commercial exchange took place. There are stitches called 'The Road to Damascus' and 'The Road to Egypt', which were embroidered onto the dresses when, for example, the *jhaz* of the bride was bought from those cities. Ironically, these joyful trips in preparation for weddings later became the same escape routes taken by refugees after the Nakba. Times had changed.

Today there is a systemic and active effort to steal and destroy the traditional thobes of Palestine in an attempt to erase or rewrite history and deny our existence. We wanted to translate the significance of this heritage and document it with a more durable material, so we decided to work with stone. We went to Italy first to a prominent stone factory hoping to collaborate with them. They said our designs were too detailed and intricate, and that it wouldn't be possible to work on their machines. We were quite disappointed; either our imagination was going too far, or we had to learn to do it ourselves.

Green Bridal Chest, 2023, Naqsh Collective.

When we were back in Amman, we started using various machines in different ways. When we finally managed to make it work, we were able to engrave very intricate and delicate details into the stone, marking a real turning point in our practice.

Stone became a big part of our story – selecting the right piece and carefully studying the grain, colour, durability and source became very important. Similar to how each thobe is unique, each stone has its own personality and reveals itself to us as we engrave or cut it.

As for the brass, we source this material from the scraps of metalsmiths' workshops, sorting it into different sizes and traits according to roughness – from the fine powder to the coarse shavings. We also experiment with polish to get different shades and gloss. We use three or four different machines in the process, and we now know what to use and how much we can stretch them to their limits.

Naqsh Collective

Artisans are often thought of as less than artists, but that is not true. Just because we are prolific makers doesn't mean we work on a production line. We see a lot of similarities between the craft we practise at Naqsh, and the way embroidery was practised in the past, and how intuitively the piece comes together. If a single stitch is removed, it removes the balance of the piece. Even if we use the same guidelines and colours, we won't ever create the same two pieces. I can make so many iterations using the same basic alphabet. That's the beauty of craft.

The Naqsh technique of engraved and carved stone with brass inlays and shavings has become our trademark and provenance. In a way, we've created a new craft. We've been able to apply the techniques across different patterns, which we research for different commissions across the region – from the *sadu* weaving of Jordan, to textiles, stone etchings, and architectural engraving patterns found in Saudi Arabia, Oman, the United Arab Emirates, etc. For each commission, we engage in the same depth of research that we did on Palestinian embroidery.

Top left: *The Oranges Chair* (Jaffa Chair), 2017, Naqsh Collective. Displayed in *A Chair Tale* at Jordan National Gallery of Fine Arts, as part of Amman Design Week 2017. Left: *Heavy Roads*, 2020 (detail), Naqsh Collective. Above: *Unit and Diaspora (Wihdeh Wa Shatat)*, 2018, Naqsh Collective. Exhibition view, *Unit and Diaspora*, 2018.

The patterns in our region never conformed to the current political borders and identities – they were attributed to vast geographic regions composed of different people and tribes. That's why there is a lot of overlap and similarities, but also different attributions to tribes or families. They tell a multitude of stories about our region – how these patterns were conceived, exchanged and evolved. What makes Palestinian embroidery unique to us is the vast collection of prototypes and multitude of variations developed over many years, and their strong associations with identity, cities and the land. This deeper meaning and connection are what we hope to share.

Right: *Green Bridal Chest*, 2023 and *Onyx Shawl*, 2023, Naqsh Collective. Exhibition view, *Arab Design Now*, 2024.
Left: *Onyx Shawl*, 2023 (detail), Naqsh Collective.

Naqsh Collective is an Amman-based design practice founded by sisters Nisreen and Nermeen Abudail. Their work repositions elements of Middle Eastern art, architecture and heritage in a minimalist frame that can also be extremely decorative, depending on the piece. Meticulously documenting patterns found in Palestinian embroidery and other textile crafts across the region, their signature stone with brass inlay designs carry stories at the crossroads of regional cultures. *Green Bridal Chest* and *Onyx Shawl* are two such pieces, with traditional Palestinian patterns depicting flora and fauna in the region, as well as preserving cultural dimensions of womanhood, marriage and family.

Dubai-based designer and interior architect Carla Baz first established her studio in Beirut, where she continues to collaborate with skilled craftspeople. Her works are at once sculptural and practical, ornate and clean, strong and subtle. Her pieces strive to redefine conventional approaches to furniture-making, experimenting with materials such as marble, resin and brass, while respecting their integrity. In the *Oyster* series of sculptural lights, Carla Baz experiments with textures, patinas and reflections, as well as the ethereal and iridescent tones of mother of pearl. The *Monarch* table lamp features flamboyant coloured marble stones, selected for their embellished texture, to achieve a sense of opulence and lightness.

Carla Baz

Below: *Minerals Console Table* and *Oyster Ceiling Mounted Lamp*, 2023, Carla Baz. Right: *Oyster Wall Mounted Lamp with Rod*, 2022, Carla Baz.

“To me design is a form of dialogue so it only makes sense that it unfolds in the form of an ongoing conversation.”

Carla Baz

Monarch Table Lamp with Dome, 2022, Carla Baz.

Tamara Barrage is a Lebanese artist and designer based in Dubai. Aspiring to better articulate how forms and textures provoke senses, manipulate emotion, and articulate memories, her work explores the tactile and sensorial characteristics of various materials. *Traces of Light*, which was first conceived while the artist was in a residency at the Schloss Hollenegg castle in Austria, is a modern interpretation of an 18th-century candelabra found at the entrance of the building. The bulbous forms were blown from coloured borosilicate glass in Beirut, with the duality in colour referencing the duality of materials found in the origin piece at Schloss Hollenegg.

Tamara Barrage

Traces of Light, 2022, Tamara Barrage.

"To create in our region, to me, is to initiate, discover, learn and teach. It's the fruit of many collaborations between makers, thinkers and dreamers."

Tamara Barrage

Traces of Light, 2022 (detail), Tamara Barrage.

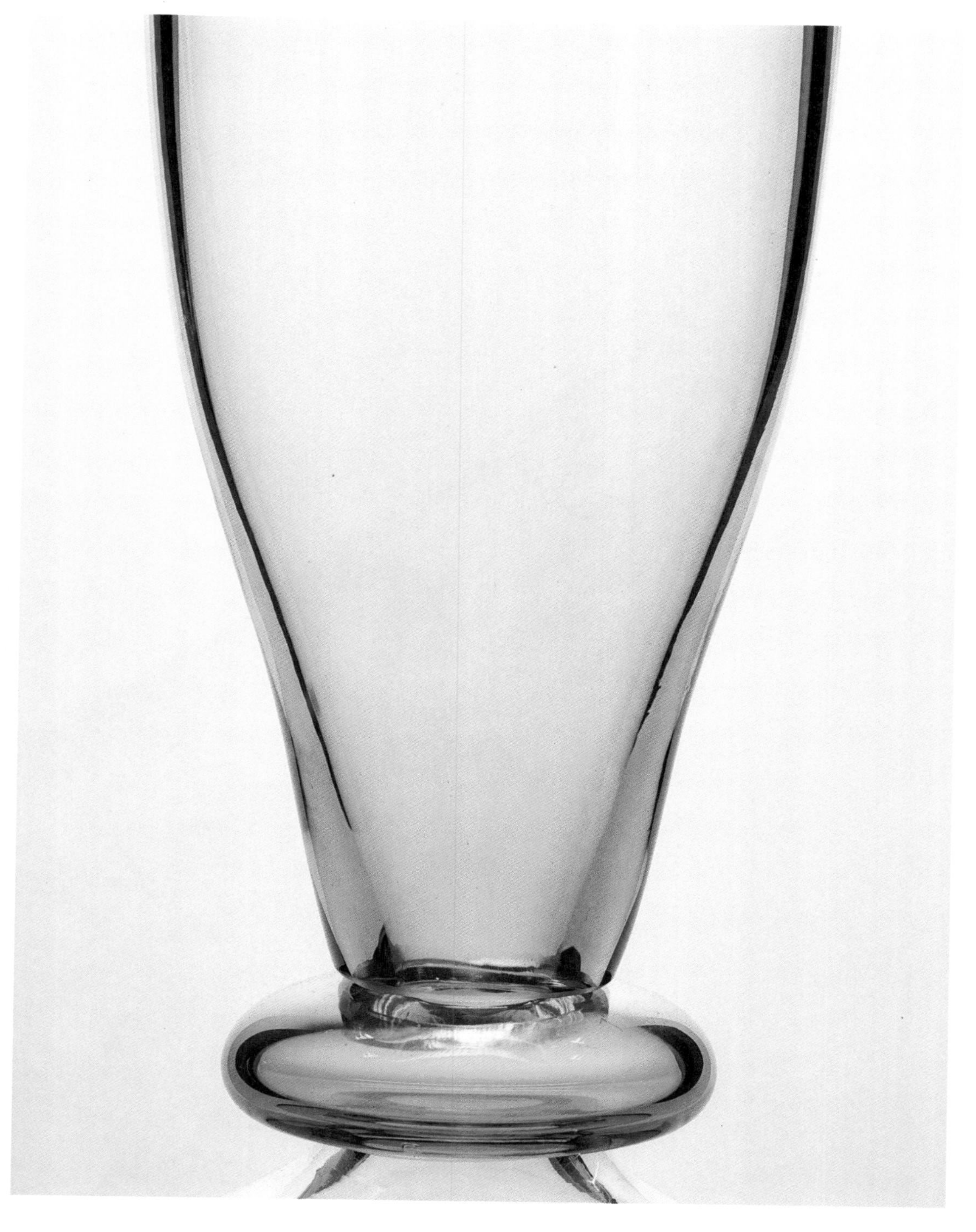

Flavie Audi

Flavie Audi is an artist and designer exploring speculative geologies and imagined post-human topographies. In a dematerialised world where all is virtual and generic, her work navigates the digital atmosphere, seeking to define a new type of aesthetic and physical materiality. *Prescient Lagoon* is part of a body of work that weaves through a geological narrative, to a speculative world where physical and virtual meet. Made from digital and handcrafted processes that combine resin, glass and lacquered fibreglass, the work is suspended between the natural and artificial.

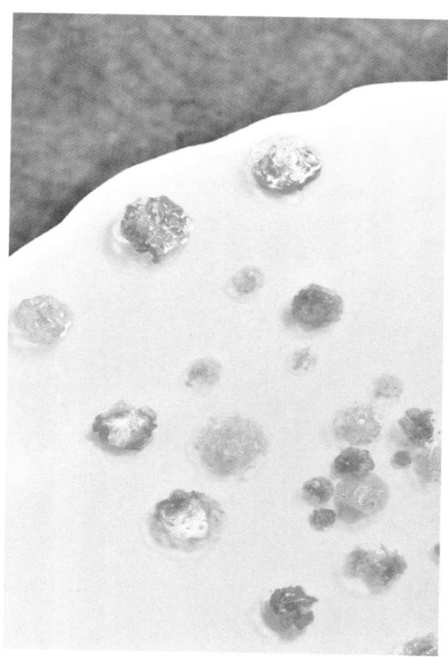

Prescient Lagoon I, 2020, Flavie Audi.

Moïo Studio is the Berlin-based ceramic atelier of French-Palestinian artist Maia Beyrouti. Her practice focuses on sculptural design and experimental glazes, based on the work of the studio's material research lab. Using forms and techniques inspired by architecture and geology, raw materials, and process, all pieces are handmade by the artist. *Roche Side Table* is constructed with a mix of wheel-thrown and hand-building techniques, whereas *Rhomboid Side Table* is completely handmade. *Blue Marble Table* is glazed using copper and locally sourced marble dust resulting in white streaks and some deeper blues where it reacts with the copper glaze.

Left: *Blue Marble Side Table*, 2023, Moïo Studio.
Above: *Rhomboid Side Table*, 2023, Moïo Studio.

Moïo Studio

"As part of the Palestinian diaspora, I can only speak in terms of what design means for me in relation to the region. Working with clay and raw materials is a reflection of my need to return to the source, to understand the land, and to create links with my ancestry."

Maia Beyrouti

Roche Side Table, 2023, Moio Studio.

Thomas Trad is a furniture and product designer from Beirut. Driven by a fascination with manufacturing processes and craftsmanship, his designs reference Japanese aesthetics and reflect a rich tapestry of cultural influences and diverse techniques, fusing history, innovation, and the spirit of the Lebanese people. *M Coffee Table* is handcrafted from high-quality oak and meticulously carved with a chisel to create an intricate *naguri* pattern. A circle, slightly off-centre, is intentionally left untouched by the chisel, creating a focal point, in contrast to the intricacy of the carving. *Alia Metal Vase* is crafted from a solid block of aluminium, milled on the inside. Polished stainless-steel rods intersect the surface, creating an interplay between the two metals.

Thomas Trad

Left: *M Coffee Table*, 2022, Thomas Trad.
Below: *Alia Metal Vase*, 2022, Thomas Trad.

"Being a designer in Lebanon is a testament to resilience and creativity, as it involves navigating a rich tapestry of cultural and diverse traditions, ultimately resulting in designs that reflect a harmonious fusion of history, innovation, and the indomitable spirit of the Lebanese people."

Thomas Trad

M Coffee Table, 2022, Thomas Trad.

Arita
Studies
in Japanese
Porcelain
PHAIDON

Aline Asmar d'Amman is an architect and founder of Culture in Architecture, a cross-disciplinary studio based between Beirut and Paris. Using hand-picked discarded marbles and brutalist slabs of Vicenza stone, the collection of functional sculptures titled *Memory of Stones* is a play between ruination and primary construction and is centred around the idea of 'concrete poetry'. The scorched surfaces and scars on the slabs are juxtaposed with the raw beauty of quarry-extracted stone and rare marble fragments. The pieces are crafted in a collaborative effort with historic-marble artisans in Vicenza, Italy.

Left: *Memory of Stones II Coffee Table*, 2020, Aline Asmar d'Amman. Above: *Memory of Stones III Desk*, 2020, Aline Asmar d'Amman.

Aline Asmar d'Amman

Stone Cloud Side Table, 2022, Aline Asmar d'Amman.

Nada Debs talks about how experimentation and play led to the creation of a contemporary craft aesthetic that resonated across the Arab World.

✦

I grew up in Japan, where there is a philosophy to always strive for something better, something closer to perfection. There is no 'satisfaction', but a constant search to achieve a higher level of practice and craft.

When I moved to Lebanon in 2000, I started to look for local furniture and crafts, and was surprised to find that most furniture was in fact imported from Europe or elsewhere. In my search, I was led to a workshop in Damascus where they created 'Ottoman-style furniture', like the ones we associate with our grandparents, full of elaborate mother of pearl inlay work. The artisans there practised their craft with a great deal of pride and dedication, and yet, the amount of patience, know-how, beauty and effort was sadly going unnoticed. It's an aesthetic that people were not interested in anymore. So I set out to find a way to translate that passion and craft and know-how in a style that people could relate to.

I believe this is where, subconsciously, my exposure to Japanese aesthetics came into the picture. Growing up in Japan, I was surrounded by master craftsmen and handcrafts were everywhere. Naturally, I picked up on the aesthetic of pure minimalist design and patterns. I realised what I wanted to do was to bring that purity to the Damascene crafts, to strip them of the decorative elements and reveal their essence. I wanted to shift the perspective of what Middle Eastern furniture could be.

Initially, I would often travel to Damascus to spend time with craftspeople and artisans, watching them work, and opening a dialogue and process. When I asked the craftsmen if they could make me a rectangular panel with simple geometries – circles, or triangles, or squares – the common response would be: 'You don't want flowers?' Then, I met a Syrian artisan in Beirut named Hussam, who specialised in restoration work. I asked him if he could inlay mother of pearl into plexiglass, and he told me to come back in three days. When I returned, sure enough, he'd found a way to do it! Anything I requested of him, he would ask me to return in three days, and he would have figured it out. This was the beginning of a beautiful relationship. Though we were creating pieces using traditional methods, I was introducing new materials like resin, plexiglass or concrete.

Studio Nada Debs

When I started this work, I didn't have an office or a brand. It was just me playing around. I had designed some furniture when I was in London, but I hadn't found my identity yet. Until then, my style might have been considered more 'Japanese' because it lacked a clear Arab identity. It was when I discovered the possibilities of using regional crafts that my work started to take on a life of its own. I called my new design approach 'East and East', and it became my mission statement: celebrating Middle Eastern craft with Far Eastern philosophy. For the first time, I felt a strong connection with the pieces I was making. The style not only resonated with me, but with other people who were starting to return to Beirut after living abroad because of the war. They were all seeking what I was seeking: a sense of connection to the past, but a contemporary sense of identity. I realised I was touching upon something very much at the core of Arab society.

Soon, I started being recognised as the one who likes to 'modernise' craft techniques, and was commissioned to produce work for institutional clients and various Arab heads of state. I believe it's because we share an idea of what it means to be Arab in this era. It is broadening what it means to 'look' Arab and allowing us to construct a more contemporary image, while staying true to our roots and traditions. The mission and high level of craftsmanship I apply in my work were strong enough to carve out my own brand.

Left: Nada working with women carpet weavers of Afghanistan for the *You and I Carpets* collection, 2016, Studio Nada Debs x FBMI. Below: *MM Table Black*, 2017, Studio Nada Debs, House of Wang.

Being in Lebanon is a big part of my practice. For a long time, there has been a global perception that the 'Western' world is where the inspirations come from. I believe that it's the Arab world, our world, where true innovation is taking place. In Lebanon, I'm seeing a new generation of designers who are not just designing, but also working by hand. There is a real return to craft and making, injected with a lot of experimentation. It's very easy to prototype in Beirut – everything is accessible, and the makers are very accommodating. Tripoli also used to be the centre for furniture making in the 1970s and '80s. There are a lot of attempts to work with the people there to keep them active and sustain their practice.

Islamic geometry is also a big part of my identity. In Islam, geometric patterns are used as an abstract manifestation of the Divine and I believe we are attracted to them because they're innate in us. Sacred geometries exist on a microscopic cellular level as well as on a macroscopic level. It is what links us, globally and universally. A major source of inspiration for me in the design process is the geometry you find in Arab architecture, which I incorporated into furniture and home accessories.

I would sit for hours studying the geometry of backgammon boards, for example, which if you examine carefully, you notice include tiny triangles, squares, circles and lines. These shapes are formed from different species of wood that produce different shades: cherry wood is more red, oak wood is more yellow, walnut is more brown. Artisans create these boards by cross-cutting the different types, and arranging them like a puzzle, with each slice making up a pattern in the board.

Watching the creation of these boards and understanding the technical work behind the craft gave me a lot of space to start experimenting. I incorporated new colours, introduced more simple stripes, simplified the arabesque patterns on the marquetry, and applied it to furniture. We would put it on the edge of tabletops or on the side of shelves. Throughout, we were searching for ways to utilise this intricate geometric technique.

After the initial experimentations with marquetry we realised something interesting: the decorative strips could bend. This meant that we could start applying the strips on rounded furniture forms, straying away from just solely linear shapes. We called these designs 'Funquetry' because we felt they were fun and funky and realised that it was important to innovate by creating new ways of working with craft that would be challenging to the artisans and also more difficult to imitate.

I am often associated with mother of pearl and inlay work because at the start of my career, I began experimenting with its traditional application to see how I could push it to another level. I introduced a 'design element' to craft. Mother of pearl actually comes in many colours: brown, abalone, almost black, and yellow. I thought of creating objects using different shades and also experimented with stains to create gradations of colour, for example, from pink to yellow to orange, as well as introducing Japanese patterns along with our Arab ones.

Left: *Arabesque Chair*, 2010, Studio Nada Debs. Above: *Classic Trays*, 2010, Studio Nada Debs. Right: *Funquetry Backgammon Board*, 2017, Studio Nada Debs.

I chose mother of pearl because it really distinguishes the Levant from the greater region. For example, Iran is known for turquoise and mirror work; India, for hand carving; and in Pakistan and Afghanistan, there's a lot of marble work. This part of the world, specifically Damascus, was the centre for mother of pearl inlay during Ottoman times. It differs from the Egyptian *safsafah*, which is a process of cutting pieces and laying them next to each other; in Damascus, it involves carving into the wood using a very malleable, rope-like material made of tin and then placing the mother of pearl inlay.

In our studio we have a lot of fun experimenting, and testing the limits of craft. I once designed a coffee table, which my son affectionately called the 'Coffee Bean Table' because of its simple elliptical shape and the black-brown colour of the Macassar ebony wood. The reason we had designed it in such a large size was because long and bulky sofas were very much in style and clients were asking for coffee tables to go with them. By adding an opening within the shape, we created a celestial looking object, with two floating pieces.

Studio Nada Debs

Left: *Gandara Table*, 2022, Studio Lel and Studio Nada Debs, sold through Galerie BSL. Above: *Now & Zen Bar Cabinet*, 2016, Studio Nada Debs.

While we originally made it in Macassar ebony using the linear grains of the wood as rays, I wanted to push the craft to its limits, re-creating this table completely with a mother of pearl inlay. The strips imitated the rays of the Macassar ebony lines, starting at around two or three millimetres, then extending to about one or two centimetres in width. It took the artisans months and around 90 kilogrammes of mother of pearl to inlay this intricate piece. It has a jewel effect with the reflection of the lustre of the material. The piece became known as the 'Bling Bling Coffee Table' because we felt that mother of pearl in our region was considered 'bling'!

Collaborations play a big role in my practice and have taken me to other regions and introduced me to new crafts. In 2017, I was invited by the Fatima Bint Mohamed Bin Zayed Initiative (FBMI) to collaborate on an initiative to empower women carpet weavers in Afghanistan, where we combined traditional patterns using a new technique. I also worked with Studio Lel in Pakistan on an experiment with marble, and in 2022 I was invited to collaborate with Irthi Contemporary Crafts Council in the UAE. Alongside four expert Emirati craftswomen, all hailing from Dibba al Hisn, we combined the traditional Emirati *talli* technique with Lebanese marquetry, to produce the *Zenobia* collection.

Though similar in appearance, *talli* and marquetry use different processes and materials. *Talli* is a meticulous hand-woven embroidery technique passed down from mother to daughter, which often finds its place in the vibrant textiles of the traditional Emirati garments. On the other hand, marquetry is predominantly a craft done by men. In our project, the *talli* gave solidity to the marquetry by binding it together yet with a supple characteristic.

The end result was a reinterpretation in solid oak of the classic copper vases and vessels carried by Bedouin tribes, weaving together two different crafts from the greater region.

My journey has been an organic one, and I am very proud of where I've come from. Initially, as my home became full of visiting clients and my bedrooms were transforming into offices, I realised I needed to establish a more accommodating studio space. I found one I loved with large windows in Saifi Village in Beirut. People could pass by and see me working and I would often receive visitors who would inquire about the few furniture pieces I had. I realised that they thought I had a retail store. In my head, I wasn't a shop. I was just a studio. I didn't work with collections and launch them for sale. Everything I did at the time was bespoke.

So later, in 2018, I decided to move to Gemmayze Street, one of the main and oldest streets in Beirut. We are currently in a building from the 1930s. It is a big apartment that feels like home with high ceilings and traditional windows. It feels like the right backdrop for our pieces. We wanted clients to have the experience of coming into a working studio and engaging with the design process. It creates a stronger connection with and understanding of the value of craft and gives a more personalised experience.

Above: *The Bling Bling Coffee Bean Table*, 2013, Studio Nada Debs.
Right: The painstaking task of applying the mother or pearl strips.

This is how we improve the perception of the value of things. I don't like the word 'luxury', but I learnt the importance of the value of craftsmanship from Japanese artisans. We consider our brand as 'high-end' because it takes a lot of hard work and dedication. The time and artistry involved needs to be acknowledged.

The value of craft can be explained as energy. When you're cooking for someone you love, and the food turns out to be so good and you can't explain it, this is normally due to the energy and devotion you are putting into it. It is almost like a meditation or an act of prayer, an act of love and care and attention. You cannot produce work using a craft, like mother of pearl, while looking away. You have to be totally immersed and focused and present. This act of love or devotion to the craft is what people feel. This is what they value.

I don't think I'm the best designer in the world, but I know that when people come, they feel something and they're drawn to it. It is this spiritual energy of devotion that the artisans project. And really there's no price you can put on that, it's priceless.

Zenobia Collection, 2022, Irthi x Nada Debs.

Studio Nada Debs

Nada Debs is a designer living and working in Beirut. Her practice spans scales and disciplines, from product and furniture design to one-off commissions across craft, art, fashion and interiors. Collaborating with artisans, she works with a variety of techniques from the region, including mother of pearl inlay, to create contemporary pieces with emotional resonance. *The Bling Bling Coffee Bean Table* features an opulent inlay of 90 kilograms of mother of pearl, every piece set by hand and seamlessly integrated into the wood of the table. In this piece, Debs has revived and taken further a labour-intensive craft that was prevalent during the Ottoman era.

Bricklab is a studio for architecture, design and experimental research based in Jeddah. Founded by brothers Abdulrahman and Turki Gazzaz, it navigates the interplay between material research, practical design, and the built environment. 6:AM is a Milan-based design brand, founded by Edoardo Pandolfo and Francesco Palù, whose glass work blends traditional artisanal methods with contemporary design. In this collaboration, the two teams created an illuminated 5-metre-tall column, titled *An Archive for Modern Glass*, which documents and recreates patterns, textures and colours used on the glass panels of modernist buildings in Jeddah in the 1960s to 1990s, when the oil economy was booming. The materials and motifs of the era are reinterpreted as contemporary design pieces crafted by Italian master artisans in Venice.

An Archive for Modern Glass, 2024. Bricklab + 6:AM. Exhibition view, *Arab Design Now*, 2024.

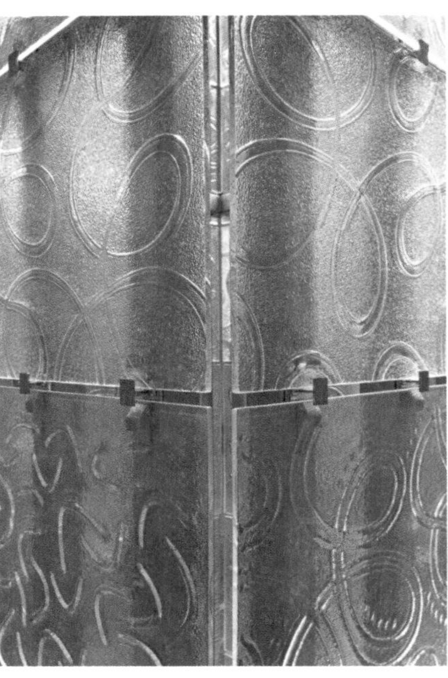

Bricklab & 6:AM

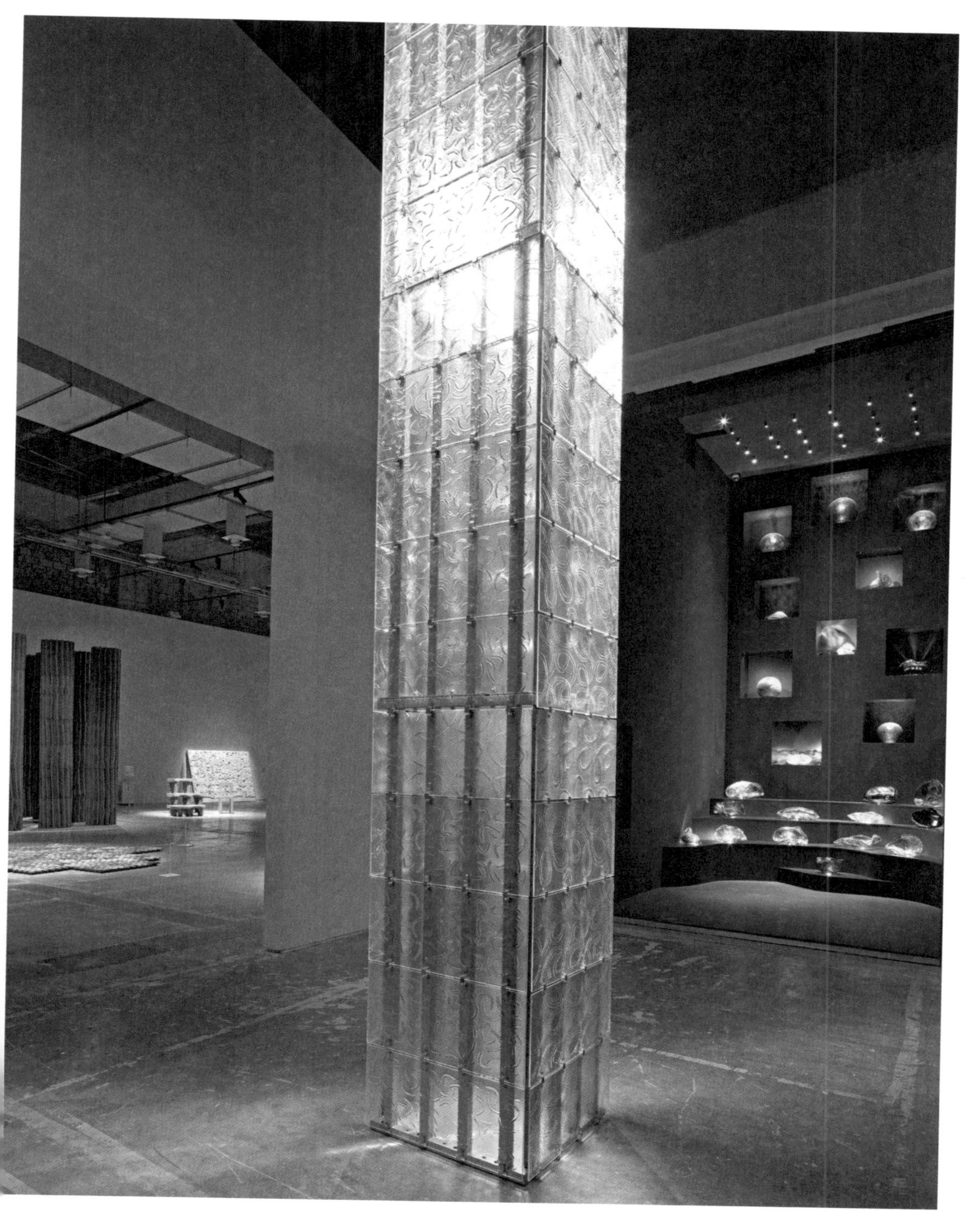

Richard Yasmine is a Lebanese interior architect and product designer. His work weaves the spirit of Beirut into minimalist designs that emerge from geometrical experimentation. Drawing inspiration from postmodernism and art deco, the *AFTER AGO* collection is crafted from diverse materials such as foam, concrete plaster and acrylic.

Richard Yasmine

AFTER AGO, 2020, Richard Yasmine.

AFTER AGO, 2020, Richard Yasmine.

david/nicolas

Constellation C080, 2018, and *B02*, david/nicolas. Exhibition view, *Arab Design Now*, 2024.

david/nicolas is a Milan-based design practice established by David Raffoul and Nicolas Moussallem. Their work in interiors, furniture, and product design combines influences from vernacular architecture, photography, electronic music, and the canon of Italian and Middle Eastern design. Their iconic *Constellation C080* dining table, a piece from their Supernova collection, is crafted from travertine slabs and adorned with intricate esoteric brass symbols. The table is set within a room featuring a *boiserie*, or modular panel system that pays tribute to the skilled craftsmen who perpetuate this artisanal trade with similar details.

Constellation C080, 2018. david/nicolas.

Karen Chekerdjian Studio

Living Space III, 2010. Karen Chekerdjian Studio. Exhibition view, Arab Design Now, 2024.

Karen Chekerdjian is an artist and designer with a diverse background in industrial, furniture, and architectural design. Her Beirut-based studio produces limited edition and custom pieces and accessories, in addition to spatial design projects. *Living Space III* is at once an architectural piece, lounger, coffee table, stool, and magazine rack. Acting as a reminder of an earlier era, the piece references modernist design from the 1920s and 1930s in shape and conception. It features the rattan panels commonly used in Lebanon to make *café-trottoir* chairs.

Filwa Nazer is a Saudi artist who works with various media including digital print, collage, textiles and the appropriation of photography. *Al Kandara Conversation 1 & 2* is an installation that explores relations between bodies and spaces, and draws on the essence of Beit Bajnaid, a modernist house built in the early 1950s in Jeddah. Employing sewing on plastic mesh screens, a play on the fragile and whimsical quality of the house, the artwork is an exploration of the aesthetic form and physical perception of this space and its transformation over time. The main feature of the screens is the hand embroidery that is reminiscent of the traditional *roshans* typical in Hijazi architecture.

Filwa Nazer

Al Kandara Conversation 1&2, 2021, Filwa Nazer.

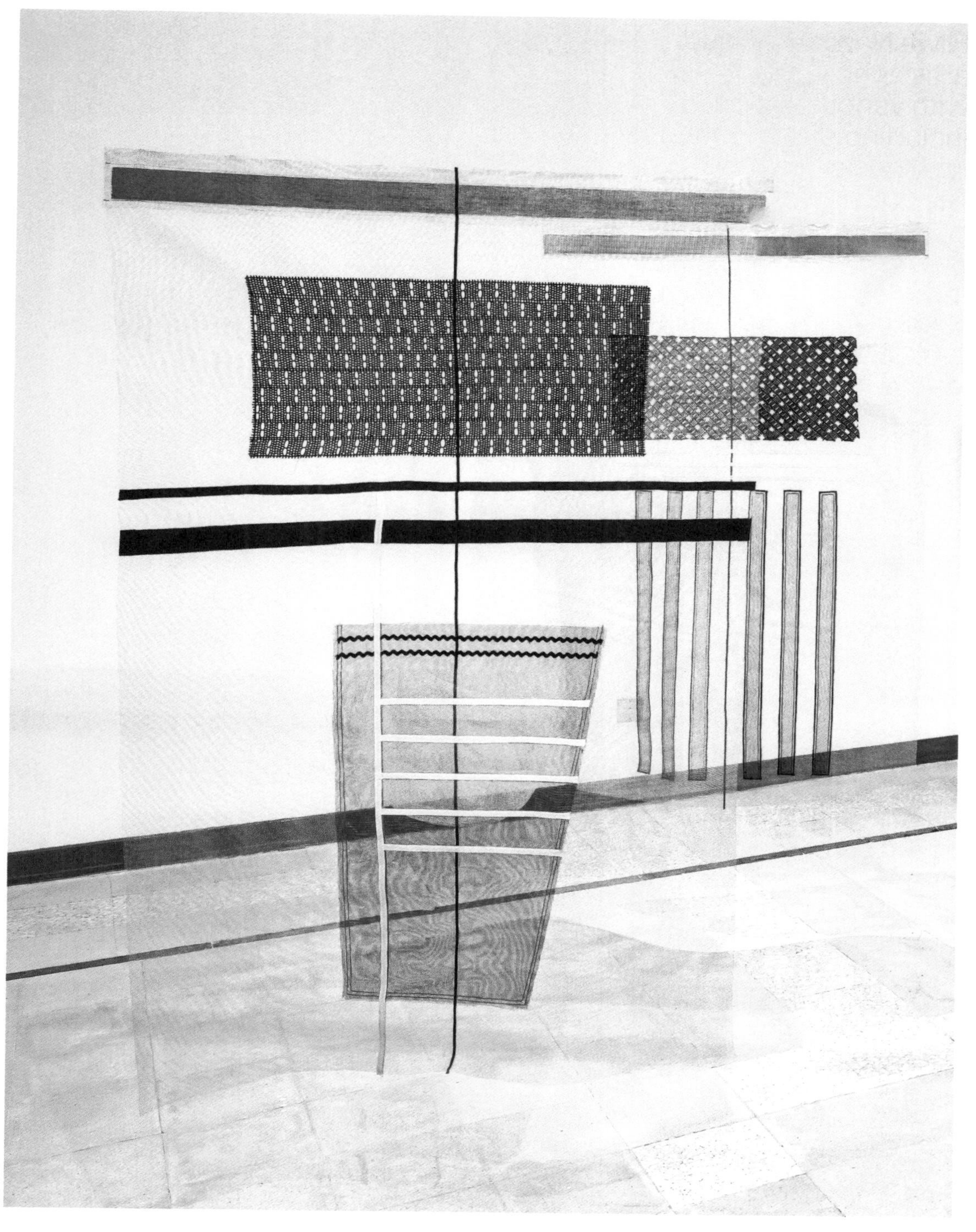

Hussein Alazaat talks about what makes the Arabic letter ✦ unique, why it became a pillar of identity and cultural unity, and how the evolution of technology influences the art form, and its delivery into the public realm.

I always talk about the Arabic letter with a sense of pride. It evolved over many years and was influenced by scripts throughout history that relied primarily on a lot of design.

The ability to record, document and communicate in written form goes back to prehistoric times. The first scripts or writing systems came out of our region – cuneiform in Mesopotamia and hieroglyphs in Egypt. The evolution of these systems from complex pictorial symbols to the development of the Arabic letter is a true revolution in design thinking. It all started roughly 3600 years ago with the important discovery of *al-Abjadiyah*, the emergence of the written language based on sounds. Suddenly, thousands of pictorial symbols were reduced to only 22 phonetic characters. It was a solution that introduced new functionality and efficiency, and opened up new possibilities; from Phoenician to Aramaic to Hebrew to Syriac, and later, of course, to Arabic, Greek, Latin and Modern European writing systems. It all started here.

Arabic is a unique script, partly instigated by the intervention of the Nabateans in the 2nd century BCE. By joining the letters together – removing the spaces between each sound and the next – they were responsible for creating the fluidity we see in Arabic today. It opened up avenues for beauty and experimentation; you could stretch the letter, extend the form or shorten it, and yet it would still be the same word. This change paved the way for Arabic writing to become an art form.

The widespread success of Arabic, of course, was due to the emergence of Islam in the early 7th century CE. It was a revolutionary time. Within the newborn Umayyad state that stretched from China to Spain, with Damascus at the centre, we now had the letter. At a time when all cultural exchange and poetry in the region relied on oral or visual transmission, this new religious expression emerged using the written word – the Qur'an. And luckily, Islam landed on a script that was already quite developed.

Just as Islam depended on the Arabic letter to spread the word of God, the Arabic letter depended on Islam to develop and flourish. Writing and re-writing the Qur'an quickly became a source of inspiration for great art. The attitude was: if I'm going to write this divine and sensitive text, I'll do so with great effort and in the most beautiful way.

As a result, Arabic scripts took on two evolving forms; Qur'anic scripts, used exclusively in writing the holy book, and non-Qur'anic scripts, used for everything else – on ceramics, plates, coins, textiles, furniture pieces, jewellery, swords, and even on grains of rice. The two types of scripts evolved as two trees branching out into many, and sometimes, tangling and intertwining into unified scripts. More often, however, there was a strong demarcation between the two types, where non-Qur'anic scripts became the vernacular, and were perceived as less pure, and the Qur'anic scripts were perceived as too rigid and lacking innovation. This classicism and competitiveness that was created 1400 years ago can still be seen today. In my opinion, without the bravery and madness of the non-Qur'anic scripts, we probably wouldn't have such a rich body of calligraphic art. They brought the letter to life.

The Arabic script evolved further with the introduction of dots and *harakat* (vowel markers), which were used to to define the letter's sound. The form itself was also largely dependent on the tools used to write. While they had access to animal hair and could make brushes, the Arabs preferred using the reed, a natural plant that grows abundantly next to rivers, which was carved to have a pointed head that could be dipped in ink. It allowed for great control and created sharp angles, allowing for contrast in the letter form – thin and thick. Interestingly, shepherds at the time also discovered that if they punched holes in a reed, it becomes a *nai*, or a flute. So music and writing in the Arab world were in fact made using the same tool.

As new scripts emerged from great cities such as Mecca, Medina, Damascus, Cairo and Baghdad, so did the experiments and exchanges. A debate was born across the region – which script was ideal for what? A *khattat* from Baghdad named Ibn Muqla, who was also a state official and a poet, was the first to set out a visual theory and rubric for the written script. He developed a way of understanding the form of the letter and its concept following specific rules; namely, using the geometry of a circle as the basic form of the letter, and setting out measurements, ratios and guidelines in his quest for the perfect form. The script we now know as the *thuluth* is one of the first examples of the cursive scripts that followed Ibn Muqla's system and philosophy

Above: Mosque Lamp, Egypt [Africa, Egypt], Sultan al-Malik al-Zahir Abu Sa'id Barquq, Mamluk (1382–1399 CE). Collection of the Museum of Islamic Art, Doha. Right: A Folio from the *Blue Qur'an*, 9th century CE, gold ink on indigo-blue coloured vellum. Collection of the Museum of Islamic Art, Doha.

surrounding the pure geometry of the circle.

The Kufic script, which denotes a kind of calligraphy that is balanced on a straight, very strong base line, first evolved in Medina, but was used and popularised by people in the city of Kufa in Iraq, with its large scribing houses. The root of this kind of script is what is called al *khutoot al yabisa* (stiff scripts), as they are tough, solid and geometric. At the opposite end of the spectrum, there were scripts known as al *khutoot al layina* (smooth scripts), which were cursive, more flowing, and not conforming to straight lines.

It is said that by the end of the 14th century there were 140 scripts, each with an intentionally different form and function. A century later, however, the Ottomans decided to reduce the number of acceptable scripts to only six or seven dominant ones, in an effort to unify tastes and define a new regional identity for the empire. It was a form of cleansing, if you will. Unfortunately, many scripts were lost; for some, all we have now are the descriptions. At the same time, artists and artisans were brought to the Ottoman capital from places like Aleppo, Damascus, Cairo and Baghdad, leaving these former springs of calligraphic art and lighthouses of knowledge in literature, chemistry, alchemy, philosophy and culture, with nothing.

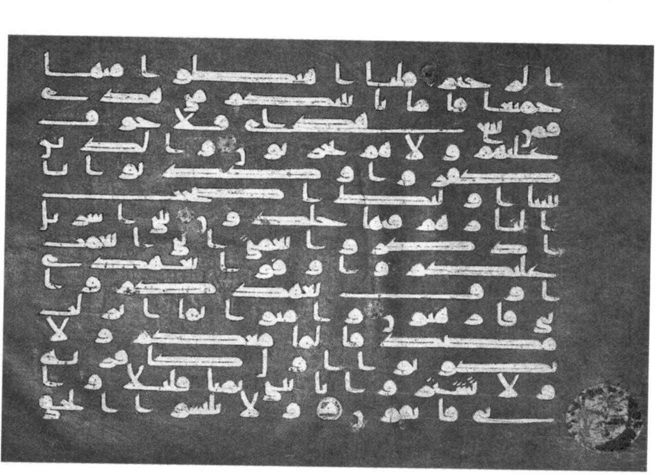

The reluctance of the Ottomans to adopt printmaking and more modern publishing tools held back the development of font styles for many years. Meanwhile in Europe, advances in technology led to the establishment of type foundries. The first Arabic letters carved on wood and cast in lead were done at the hands of Europeans hoping to spread the word of the Bible. With their untrained hands and lack of knowledge, the medium held the art form back. To this day, when I look at a font, I can sometimes see traces of the experiments done in Europe or by the Ottomans – some of which I believe included incorrect decisions. Even when printing was permitted, the Ottomans insisted it could only be used for Christian books, and not the holy Qur'an.

Scripts saw a new light with the emergence of new technologies. Creative avenues in the Arab world opened up at the end of the 18th century, when a new, more progressive Ottoman ruler brought a printing press to Istanbul. Mohammad Ali, the Ottoman governor in Cairo from 1805 to 1849, also set up a press and started manufacturing typefaces, in an effort to reignite a cultural awakening in the region which would eventually lead to a renaissance in Arabic literature and the visual arts in the late 19th and 20th centuries.

The 1960s and 70s in particular was a period of great activity in print production and design. For example, a classical *khattat* in Syria by the name of Mahmoud Hawwari designed unique dry transfer letters. In his work, he would write 'All rights reserved – Mahmoud Hawwari – Damascus', which shows that he was conscious of the importance and rarity of what he was doing. There was also great competition and innovation in the design of newspapers, especially in Beirut, and political and culture magazines championed the use of original fonts, created by such pioneers as Munir Sha'arani and Emile Min'em.

It is through the pages of these magazines and in the curves of these scripts that I developed my fascination with the Arabic letter. Growing up in the 1980s, my world was a children's magazine called *Majid*. Within its pages, I found articles, comics, and letters that filled me with anticipation and wonder. It is through *Majid* that I met my life-long mentor, artist and writer Mohieddine El-Labbad. Unfortunately, he passed away before I had the chance to meet him in person, but he had a unique talent for captivating young people, making them laugh and think, and drawing their attention to details in graphic design: the letters, floral elements, figures, architecture, iconography and imagery.

Labbad would include a weekly book review, called *khazanet al-kutub al-jamila* (the beautiful books trove). It featured a collection of books on art, culture, history, museum catalogues, and so on. As I grew older, I started my own collection of graphic design works and books from the Arab world, and eventually realised my dream

Hussein Alazaat

of establishing my own *khazanet al-kutub al-jamila*, currently located in what I call Elharf House in Amman. The space is at once a public library and a place for exchange and rich cultural immersion. It is also my studio where I do everything – design, art, collect books, document, meet people, and give workshops. I gave it that name because *el harf*, 'the letter', is the centre of my orbit. The prophet Mohammad said *la khair fi katem 'elm* (there is no good in one who withholds knowledge). If you have knowledge, you have a responsibility to share it. Like my mentor, I use modern communication tools to share parts of the library and shed light on the art of book making.

Another source of inspiration for me when I was growing up was the beautiful sign painting of the era. When I was 14, I decided during my summer break to go to a *khattat* in Amman, and there I met Haroun, who became my second life-long mentor. Through him, I learned the first basic rules of the *khatt*. It was an eye-opening experience because it was a new world where many people, artists and calligraphers, would come together.

At that time Egypt was quite developed in terms of street signage, as of course were Damascus, Baghdad and Beirut also. Painted signs became part of the urban visual scene, and a new source of experimentation – using colours, icons, symbols, drop shadows, etc, and applying them to storefronts and packaging. Now there were a lot more design decisions to make; it was a new form of public art. A new profession was born, that of the sign painter.

Sadly, the sign painters of old have become today's sign makers, and in this new 'industry' there is no room for designers. It is unfortunately not done with any artistry, having become more of a mechanical process. This was exacerbated by the computer, which made it easier to make signs quickly using badly designed fonts.

I spend a lot of time going around cities appealing to shop owners not to change their signs, to keep them intact. I started a small project where I document and share signs found in Jordanian streets, and created an Instagram page called *Jordanian Khatt*. I enjoy showing how *khatt* is used in popular culture, born out of a total lack of awareness of any rules and sometimes very inspiring and liberating.

Left: Sample sheets of dry transfer letters.
Above: *Majid* magazine, 1979.

The city's storefronts are not the property of the shop owner alone, but also of the city's residents; they carry the city's identity and culture, as well as a feeling of the industry, professions, and crafts that the city is home to. Storefronts became my canvas, through which I could share my passion for Arabic lettering.

In 2012, I cofounded a project called Wajha, which aims to bring together designers and small businesses who would otherwise resort to going to a sign maker. Our initiative was to present a storefront design and brand for free. For me, it was about getting these small businesses, whether it was a tailor, barber, or otherwise, to begin to appreciate design. It was an exchange from one professional to another.

Through Wajha and other 'public design' initiatives, I hope to produce good visual content for future generations. I especially like working with children. Instead of the usual drawings of a house, tree and sun, we assign them the role of being the graphic designer for a small business of their choice. We ask them: What will you name it? What will the logo look like? What does the storefront look like? How do we use icons or lines to showcase what the shop is about, what it offers, what the features are? This exercise goes through colours, letters and drawing icons, and the results are always great.

Western companies were the first to produce digital Arabic fonts and dominate the taste. But today, we find young designers from Morocco, Saudi Arabia and Egypt, all designing fonts. Some people do it for free and some for a fee. I can say we are now in a great position. Any Arabic website or newspaper we open today will contain a lot of unique fonts, mostly designed by Arabs. The know-how is also more available. The rules are better established, although we still don't have proper standards or guidelines that determine what is correct and what isn't. It all comes down to personal efforts.

Covers from the *Qaws Qouzah* (Rainbow) book series, written and illustrated by Arab novelists and artists and published by Dar Al-Fata Al-Arabi from 1974 to late 1980s.

Of Letters and Coins, 2021, Hussein Alazaat. Installation, National Museum of Saudi Arabia, Riyadh.

The Beautiful Books Trove, 2024, Hussein Alazaat. Exhibition views, *Arab Design Now*, 2024.

Hussein Alazaat is a multidisciplinary designer, bookmaker, curator and calligraphy artist. He is dedicated to showcasing the Arabic visual landscape, and facilitating knowledge exchange by engaging in exhibitions, publication design, archives and education. In an homage to modern-era graphic design and typography from the Arab world, *The Beautiful Books Trove* is an installation that draws from Hussein Alazaat's archiving project of the same name, currently housed in Amman. The educational space offers a curated selection of reproductions of children's publications from the 1960s, 70s, and 80s.

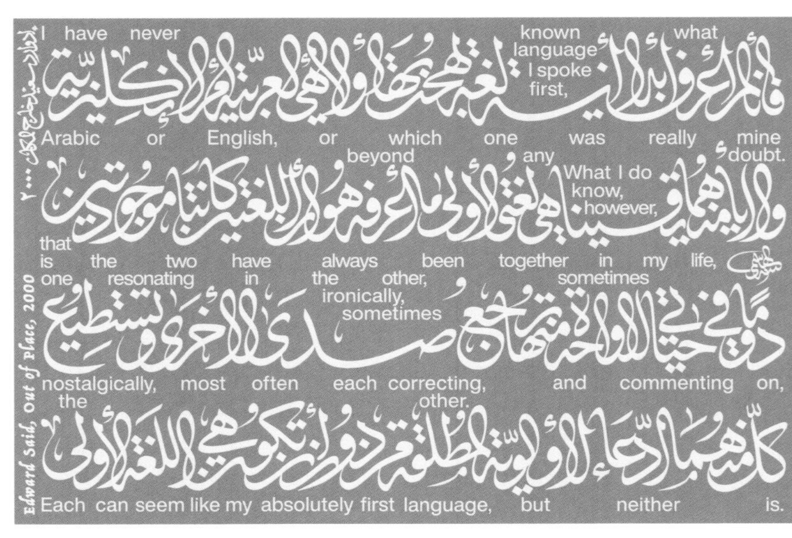
I have never known what language I spoke first,
Arabic or English, or which one was really mine beyond any doubt.
What I do know, however,
that is the two have always been together in my life,
one resonating in the other, sometimes ironically, sometimes
nostalgically, most often each correcting, and commenting on, the other.
Each can seem like my absolutely first language, but neither is.
Edward Said, Out of Place, 2000

A Woven Mimesis, 2024, 40MUSTAQEL.
Exhibition view and detail, *Arab Design Now*, 2024.

40MUSTAQEL

40MUSTAQEL is an independent design studio based in Cairo. The practice attempts to dissect and understand the complexities of a diverse Arab visual language, and is driven by the challenge of transforming the perception of design as an apolitical discipline. Their hand-knotted carpet, *A Woven Mimesis*, is crafted by skilled Egyptian artisans from the Kiliim Collective in the village of Abees, Alexandria, and features the words of Palestinian-American author Edward Said, critiquing the sentiments of estrangement towards one's own tongue (Arabic) as well as uncertainty surrounding cultural identity, heritage and linguistic experience. The text was reproduced from the hand-drawn Arabic script executed in collaboration with Yemeni calligrapher Zaki Alhashimi.

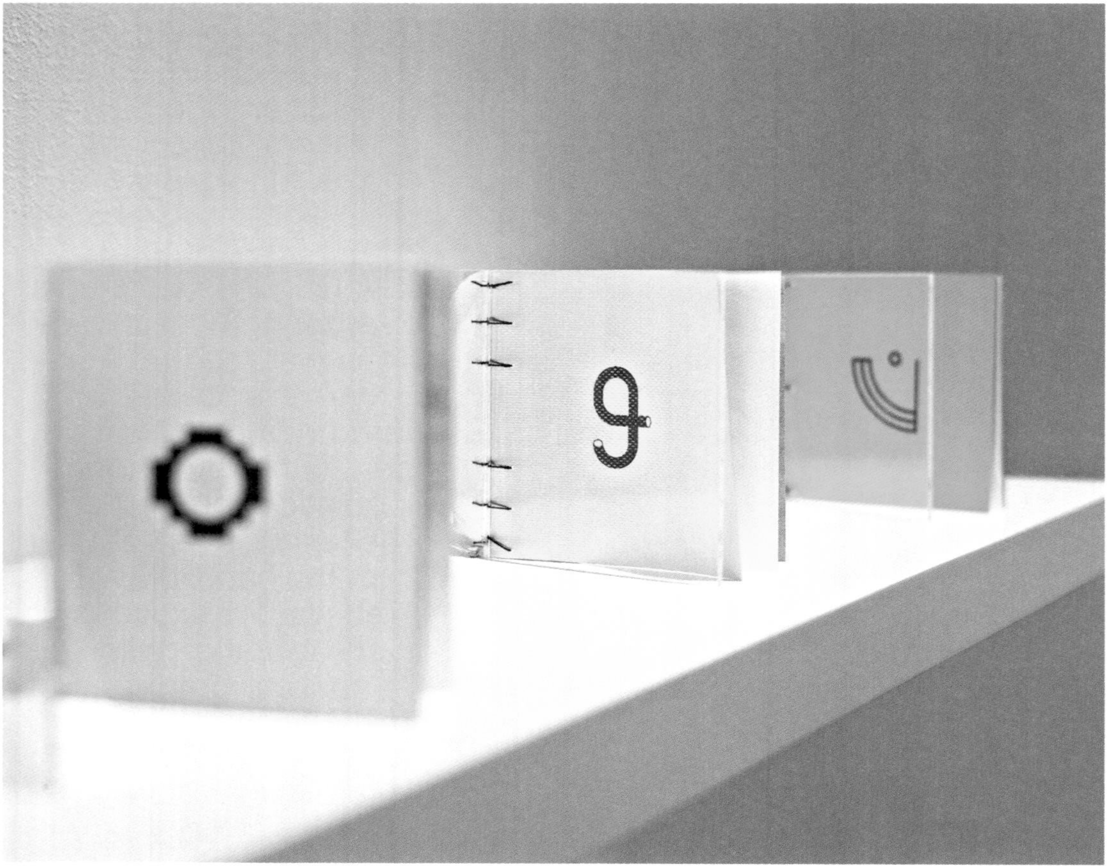

Nora Aly

Nora Aly is an independent designer and a professor at the American University in Cairo. She integrates Arabic typography in her creative projects, engaging with language as the core element shaping our collective identity. For this project, she explores the Arabic language and values through three typographic booklets, *Nun Al Niswa* (translating to N of the Female), *Waw Al Jama'a* (translating to the O of the Group), and *Al Sukoun* (translating to Serenity of Silence).

Beyond the Arabic Alphabet, 2014, Nora Aly.

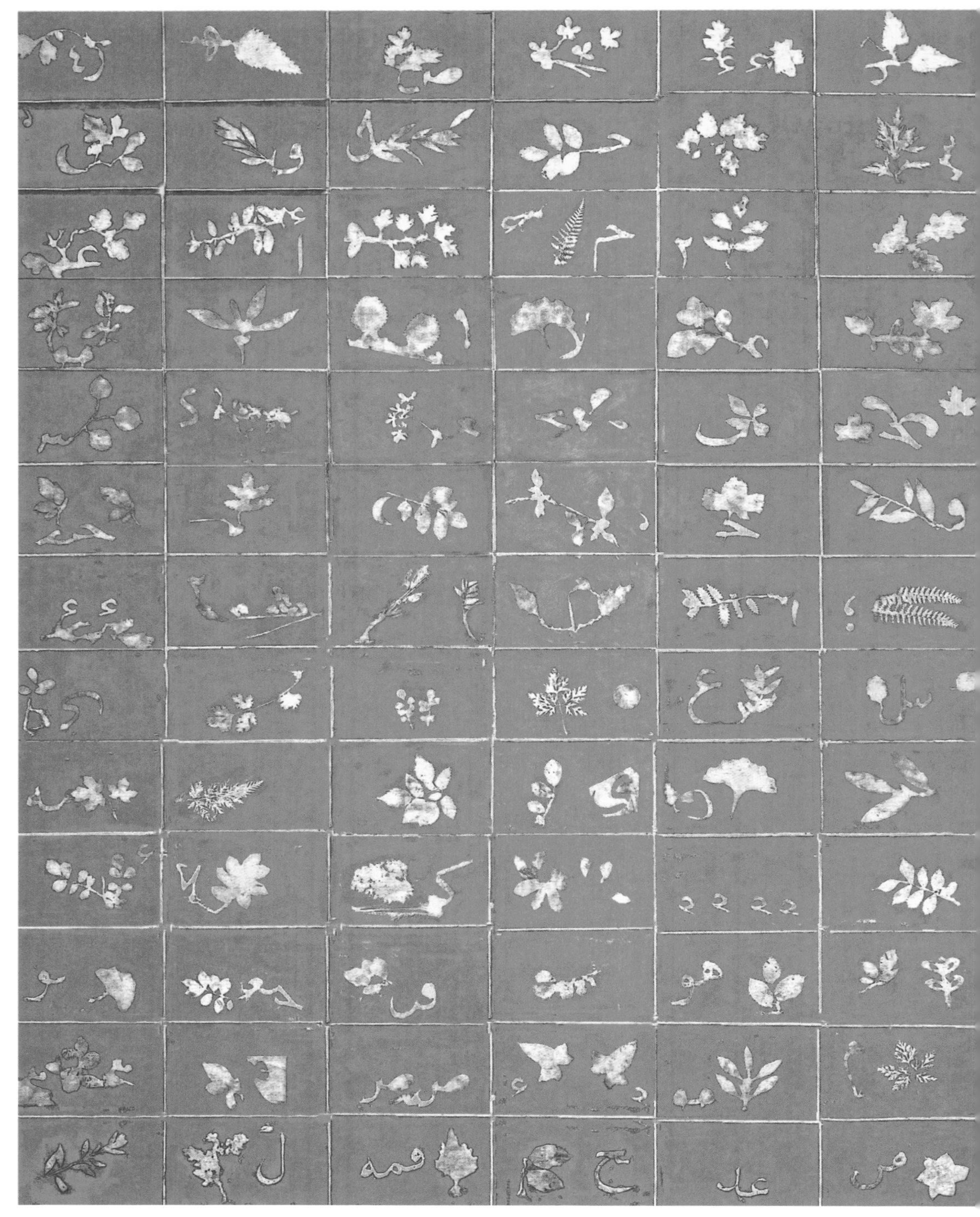

The Red Keyboard, 2023. Nedim Kufi.

Nedim Kufi is an Iraqi-Dutch graphic and multimedia designer based in the Netherlands. His work combines the Arabic language with minimalist visual concepts created for street art and land art projects. *The Red Keyboard* is a stencil oil painting on textile that introduces a new speculative language for digital communication based on plant materials foraged from daily walks in the garden.

•

Nedim Kufi

Sherine Salla

Sherine Salla is a Cairo-born designer and researcher, currently based in Amsterdam. Her practice lies in conversation with subjective histories and geographies, namely those connected to the Arabic language. *They Bore Their Names on Their Faces* investigates Arabic-language datasets housing 'Arab(ic) names' used to train natural language models (AI) in cases such as immigration control, intelligence analysis, and law enforcement. The design of this piece is inspired by passport documents as well as traditional genealogical manuscripts, a form of mapping that narrates or describes family trees and kinship linkages and is often used as a reference to learn about societies, local cultures and traditions.

They Bore Their Names on Their Faces, 2024, Sherine Salla. Exhibition view and detail, *Arab Design Now*, 2024.

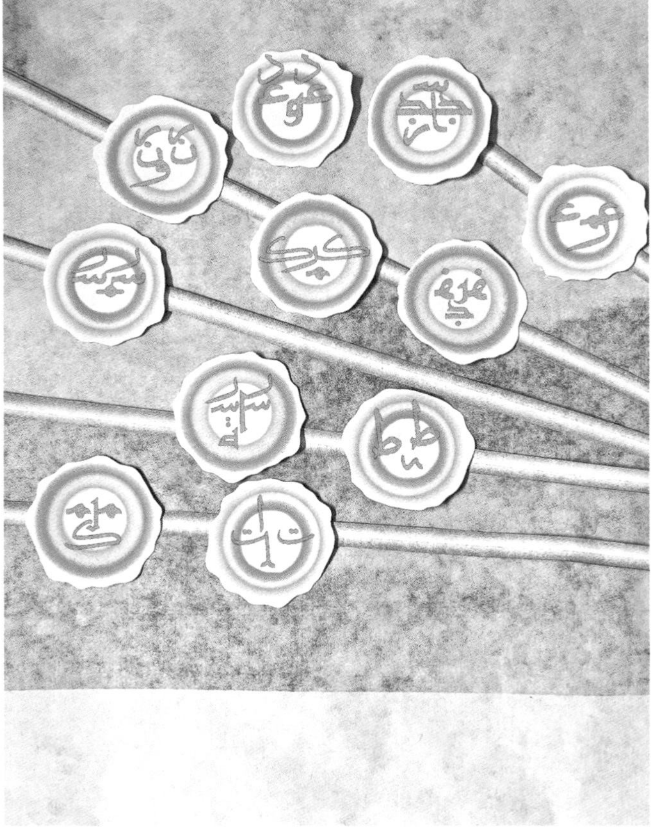

Noor Alwan is a Bahraini multidisciplinary architect and experimental artist, who utilises art as a placemaking tool, creating installations that transform physical spaces into emotional landscapes for connection and reflection. *Sacred Spaces* is a hanging installation that features various embroidered patterns, taken from a style of drawing practised by the artist's grandfather. What started as an individual introspective experiment developed into a shared family activity that entailed a collective meditation.

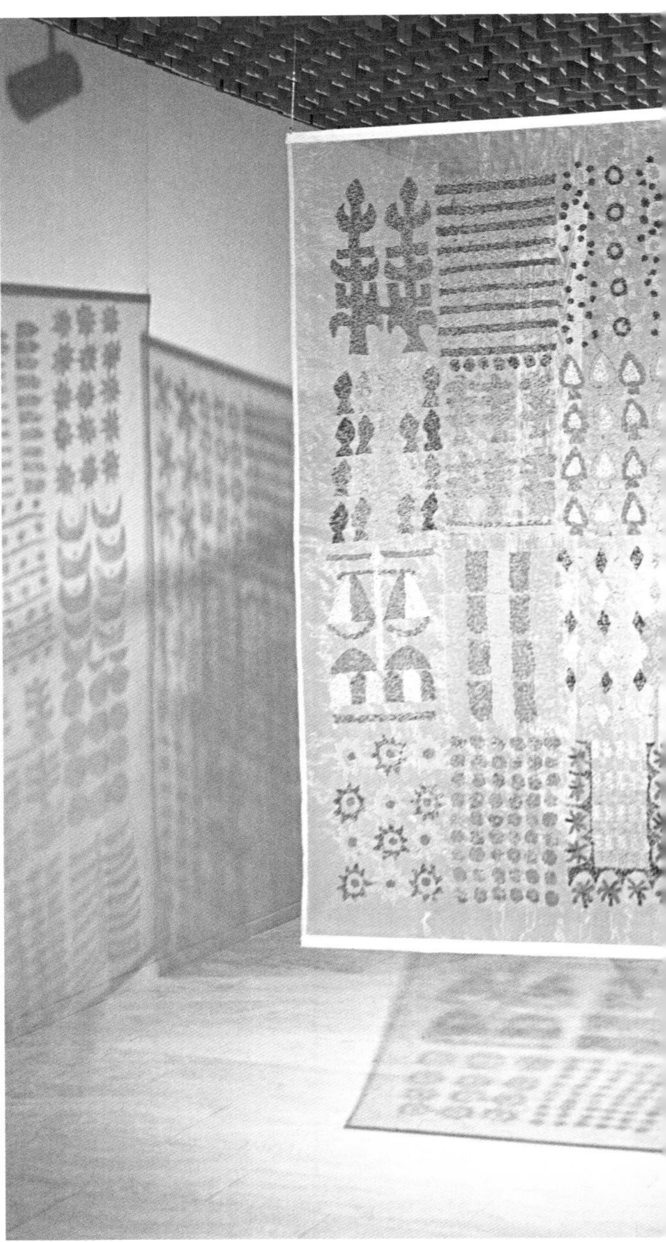

Sacred Spaces, 2021, Noor Alwan.

Noor Alwan

Designer Little empowers children's creativity by bringing their drawings alive as three-dimensional wonders. Their work fuses craftsmanship and playful imagination in celebration of children's art. In *Whimiscal Tuft*, a child's sketch is turned into a rug, which brings forth the vibrant world of four-year-old Angelina's imagination. A symphony of oranges, blues and purples intertwine, echoing the boundless horizons of youthful ingenuity.

Whimsical Tuft, 2023, Designer Little.

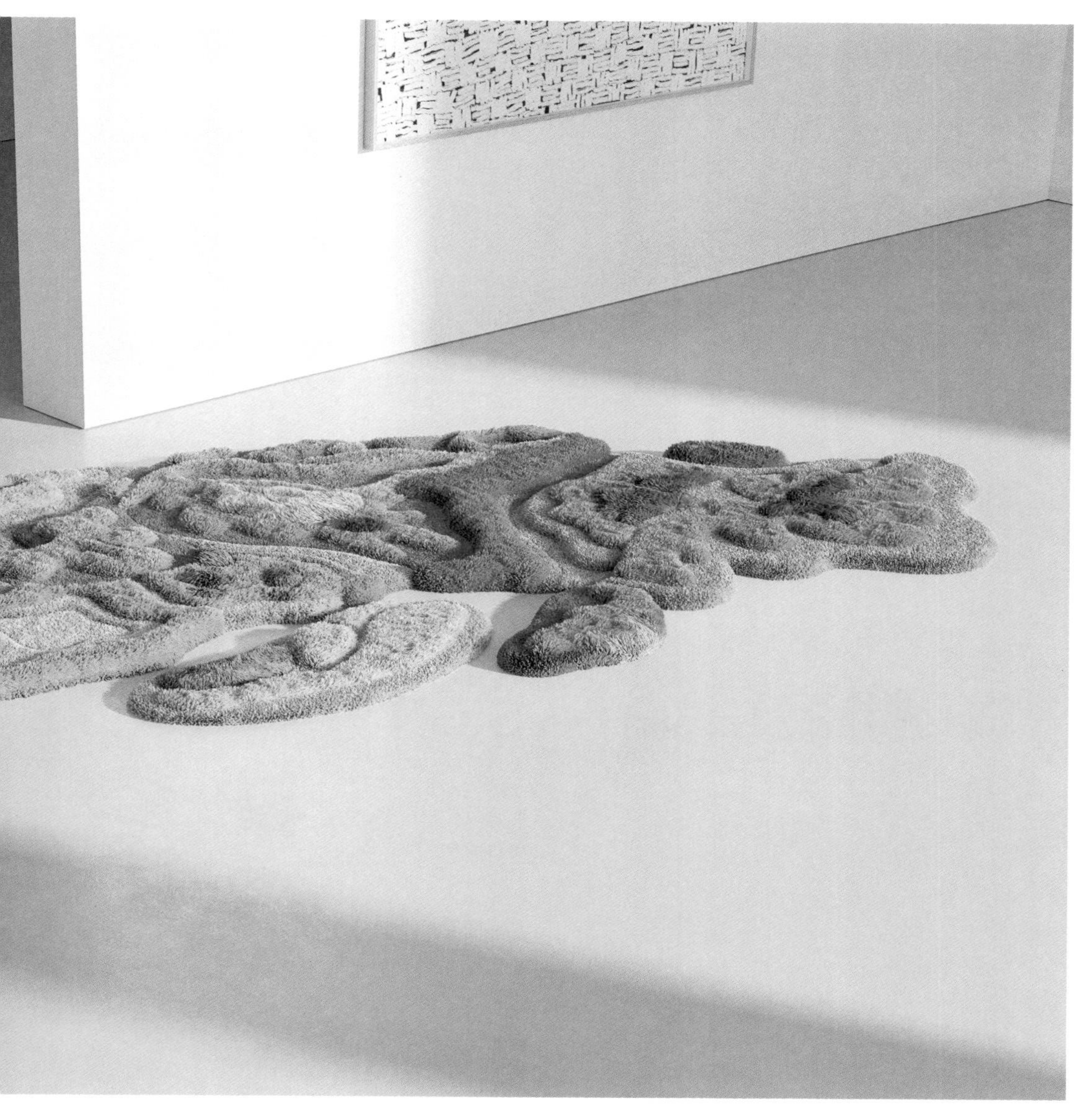

Anastasia Nysten is a Lebanese-Finnish designer who bases her design practice between Beirut and Madrid. Her furniture pieces blur the line between art and design, blending industrial production and artisanal craftsmanship. In the *Troll* collection, deconstructivism marries amorphic softness with a wooden structure, hand-carved by artisans, acting as the skeleton for loosely stacked pillows.

Anastasia Nysten

Above and right: *Troll Bench*, 2018, Anastasia Nysten.
Far right: *Troll Chair*, 2017, Anastasia Nysten.

The trio from **Mobius Design Studio** reflect on how the discipline of graphic design is expanding, and what this growing practice propels in terms of social and cultural impact.

Our practice started in a very similar way to the humble beginnings of countless small studios: grappling with how to make this 'design thing' work within the labyrinth of career, growth, life. We met at the American University of Sharjah when we were doing our undergraduate studies; Hadeyeh and Hala in visual communication (also known as graphic design), and Riem in multimedia design. We came together after graduation because we realised we had similar ambitions and work ethics quite early on. We liked to work with our hands, we were always the last people to leave the studio, and we always left behind a big mess!

After graduating in 2010, and after going through serious existential blues, feeling very constrained by the definition of a steady corporate job — sandpaper against our spirit – we decided to embark on a more experimental career trajectory. We were young, afraid and naïve, but we sought to carve out a unique space for ourselves. How could we be credible, have a wealth of self-initiated projects, learn but also earn a living? Who was going to help? Practicality necessitated engagement with commercial work to sustain our studio, but over the last 13 years, we have become more selective, gravitating more towards cultural institutions as clients. We were one of the first studios to be supported by Tashkeel, an incubator of visual art and design based in the UAE that supports designers and artists.

In 2012, we created Design House, a platform for ourselves and other practitioners in the region who were similarly interested in making and exhibiting work that is purely driven by curiosity and experimentation. We put on various collective exhibitions over the multiple editions of Design House, debuting first as part of Sikka Art Fair, and evolving in subsequent years to become part of Dubai Design Week and other events. With each exhibition, we created a publication that went beyond being a simple catalogue showing the exhibited works; each was content-rich, with commissioned essays that anchored the subject matter we were researching at the time.

When the pandemic hit in 2020, we embarked on an undertaking, still in its formative stages, that represents perhaps the most ambitious effort we've ever pursued. The Looming Council aspires to create an online digital portal that serves as a resource for educators, designers, students and researchers looking to access content

consequently, we risk
dismiss
refusal
rejecti
Perhaps we need a more wide definition of so-called failure

and graphic design references from the region that have been historically marginalised within the global graphic design canon. For the three of us, this portal is a sanctuary. It is what we would have liked to gift our younger 18-year-old selves. Sadly, what we are gathering never made it to the fringes of any class we ever took. We are guided by the resolve to remedy some of that, shedding light on the underappreciated and often overlooked voices that have shaped the graphic design landscape of our region.

The Looming Council's current focal point is the Graphic Library, a collection of extracted visual artefacts, as we call them, from local and regional archives. We are particularly interested in work conducted by the generations of graphic designers and illustrators practising between the 1930s and 1980s. When we come across a visual, logo, or interesting use of typography, we vectorise it and remove it from its context, reducing it to its basic form. These artefacts are in fact extremely rich and reflect a very different understanding of graphic design from the one we have today. Despite our own misconceptions, we have unearthed a vibrant legacy of experimentation and freedom among these graphic designers, less bound by convention than our generation. They were more in touch with their hands and with their senses than we are, and that's because they had to be.

Recent advancements in technology have resulted in certain conveniences, which perhaps don't always serve us. Today, things need to be done quickly, they need to be submitted *yesterday*, and there's always something getting in the way; for us, a deliberate slowness is important. We enjoy working with our hands and crafting things before moving them to the digital realm. We always try to heighten our haptic sensitivity because this really elevates our creativity. To us, the materials and physical attributes of a book or a printed piece are as important as the visual graphic.

We can only attribute these attitudes to how we've been trained academically. We recognise that our education was highly westernised and had very few local references. Despite the fact that we work in a region that speaks at least two languages, and operates with a minimum of two scripts, our education was strictly centred around Latin conventions. We started our careers never having worked with Arabic and

Not (Yet) Defeated poster, 2023, Mobius Design Studio.

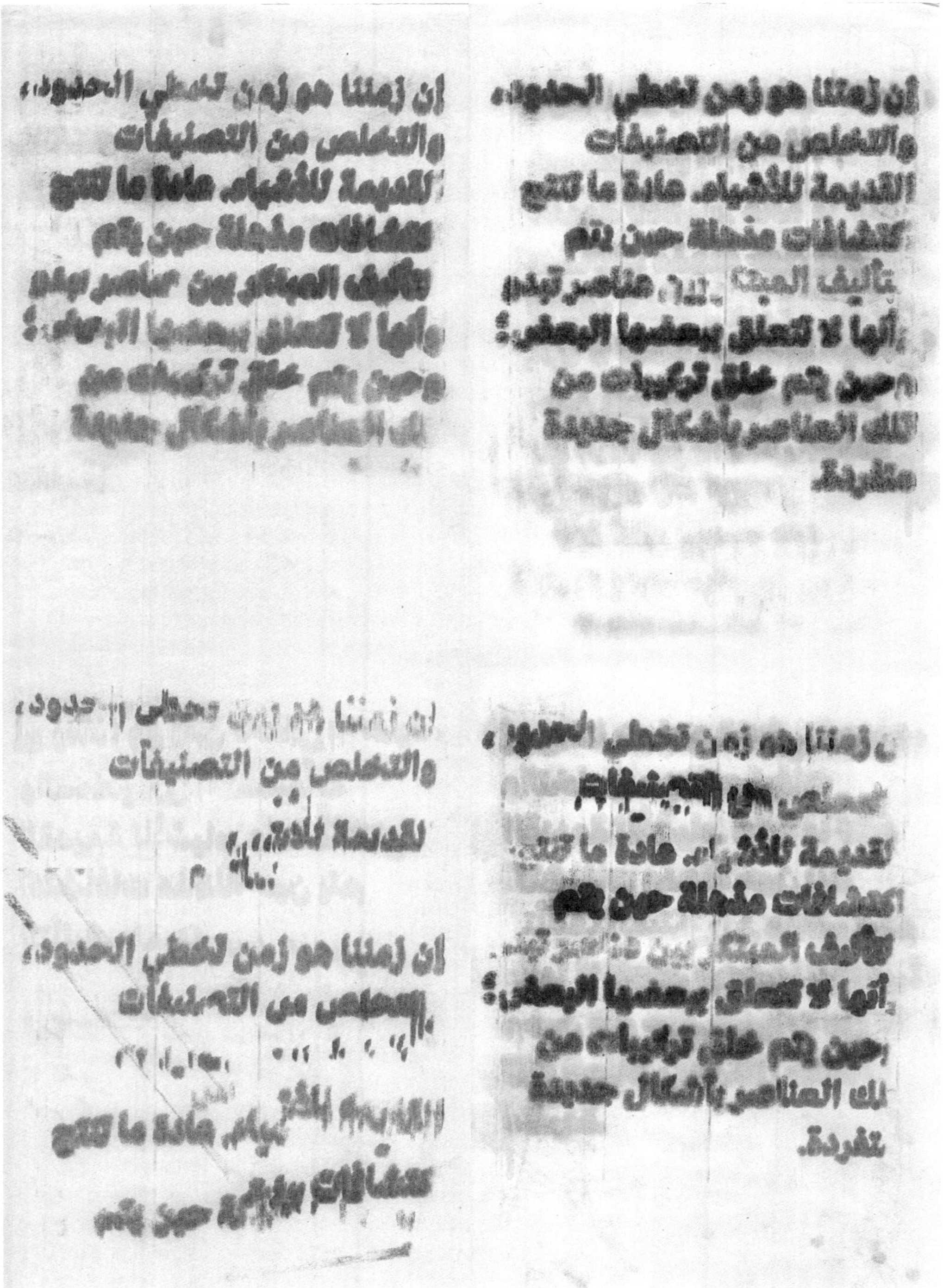

إن زمننا هو زمن تخطي الحدود،
والتخلص من التصنيفات
القديمة للأشياء. عادة ما تنتج
اكتشافات مدهشة حين يتم
تأليف المبتكر بين عناصر تبدو
أنها لا تتعلق ببعضها البعض؛
وحين يتم خلق تركيبات من
تلك العناصر بأشكال جديدة
متفردة.

إن زمننا هو زمن تخطي الحدود،
والتخلص من التصنيفات
القديمة للأشياء. عادة ما تنتج
اكتشافات مدهشة حين يتم
تأليف المبتكر بين عناصر تبدو
أنها لا تتعلق ببعضها البعض؛
وحين يتم خلق تركيبات من
تلك العناصر بأشكال جديدة

إن زمننا هو زمن تخطي الحدود،
والتخلص من التصنيفات
القديمة للأشياء. عادة ما تنتج
اكتشافات مدهشة حين يتم
تأليف المبتكر بين عناصر تبدو
أنها لا تتعلق ببعضها البعض؛
وحين يتم خلق تركيبات من
تلك العناصر بأشكال جديدة
متفردة.

إن زمننا هو زمن تخطي الحدود،
والتخلص من التصنيفات
القديمة للأشياء

إن زمننا هو زمن تخطي الحدود،
والتخلص من التصنيفات
القديمة للأشياء، عادة ما تنتج
اكتشافات مدهشة حين يتم

struggling to understand how the two scripts should function together, and this drastically hindered our ability to practise here. As students, our exposure to Arabic typography was strictly limited to looking at manuscripts and sacred texts, so when we graduated we had a 'phobia' about experimenting with Arabic letters because there was some sort of 'sacredness' associated with them. It took us a long, long time to get over it.

This is why we built opportunities like Design House and the Looming Council. Luckily, we found a synergy with other studios and individuals with similar ambitions across the region. In 2018 Fikra Graphic Design Biennial in Sharjah was launched under the theme 'Ministry of Graphic Design'. We were invited to curate one of the departments within this fictional Ministry, which was called 'The Department of Flying Saucers'. We developed the idea of 'flying in' design studios and collectives, like ourselves, who initiate exhibitions or programs, and handing over the space to them for a week with full freedom to activate it with a program or exhibition they deemed worthy. The exhibition spanned a month and was completely transformed each week by the different participants' activities. It became a series of case studies for what other practices would do in our shoes, given access to the right resources.

Turbo, a design studio based in Jordan, were mostly interested in collecting memorabilia and artefacts related to the building we were exhibiting in, a historical property that was under the threat of demolition. They used their collected objects to tell the story of the place, while also programming a series of screen-printing events highlighting some of these artefacts. Foundland Collective, a design studio based between Amsterdam and Cairo, were interested in developing alternative methods for narrating the stories of Syrian migrants, and programmed a mapping workshop for a street in Sharjah inhabited mainly by Syrians who had fled the war. On another note, Public Fiction flew in from Los Angeles, and were largely invested in making publications around the intersection of pop culture and graphic design. They transformed the space into an exploration of a publication in the making, highlighting bizarre events like Michael Jackson's visit to the UAE a decade ago, and the rumours around his desire to convert to Islam.

Left: *Silhouette, Altered*, 2018, Mobius Design Studio.
Below: *Evaporating Suns*, 2023, Mobius Design Studio.

شموس متبخرة
Evaporating Suns
أساطير معاصرة من الخليج العربي
Contemporary Myths from the Arabian Gulf
HATJE CANTZ

These projects, like our own, are an indication that attitudes to graphic design in the Arab world are radically changing. When we were in design school, it was presented as a mere marketable skill or a means to sell stuff and make others money. But in our experience, being a graphic designer today transcends being a visual communicator, it's about acting as a social agent, one who utilises intellectual and creative capabilities to advocate for important issues. It inevitably comes with greater responsibility to critically engage in research and scholarship. Today, students are starting to develop this expanded view of graphic design, using their practice to navigate the world with a sense of discernment and a zeal to drive change.

We often discuss the relationship between graphic design, or design in general, and craft. We question why certain crafts are studied formally in an academic context while others are not, when all potentially possess graphic qualities. This is the case, for example, with embroidery. We would like to adopt alternative new media and processes into our works to show that just because you're a graphic designer, doesn't mean you have to limit yourself to screen printing and digital printing. The boundaries of graphic design are ever-evolving, fluid and flexible.

It is this line of thought that led us to developing our latest project around Fareej al Marar, a famous *fareej*, or neighbourhood, in old Dubai, which all Emiraties once knew as the place to visit if you wanted to get a *jallabiya* made or embroidered. It is also a well-known fact, when shopping on that street, that using the smallest beads implies higher value and elegance. Small beads are the hardest, most labour intensive to apply to cloth, which means you need more beads to fill a small area. The more beads, the more intricate and opulent the dress.

When you go to a store, you are first welcomed by the shopkeeper and then immersed in an exquisite array of fabrics, meticulously lined up embroidered templates, and piles of sample books. However, amid this sensory overload, the craftspeople themselves are nowhere to be seen. They are invisible, as is the act of making. This, for us, is quite alarming. The need to highlight this paradox of the seen and the unseen became pressing in the aftermath of the collaboration between Dior and the Mumbai-based atelier Chanakya School of Embroidery for its pre-fall 2023 collection. In this line, Dior was collaborating with

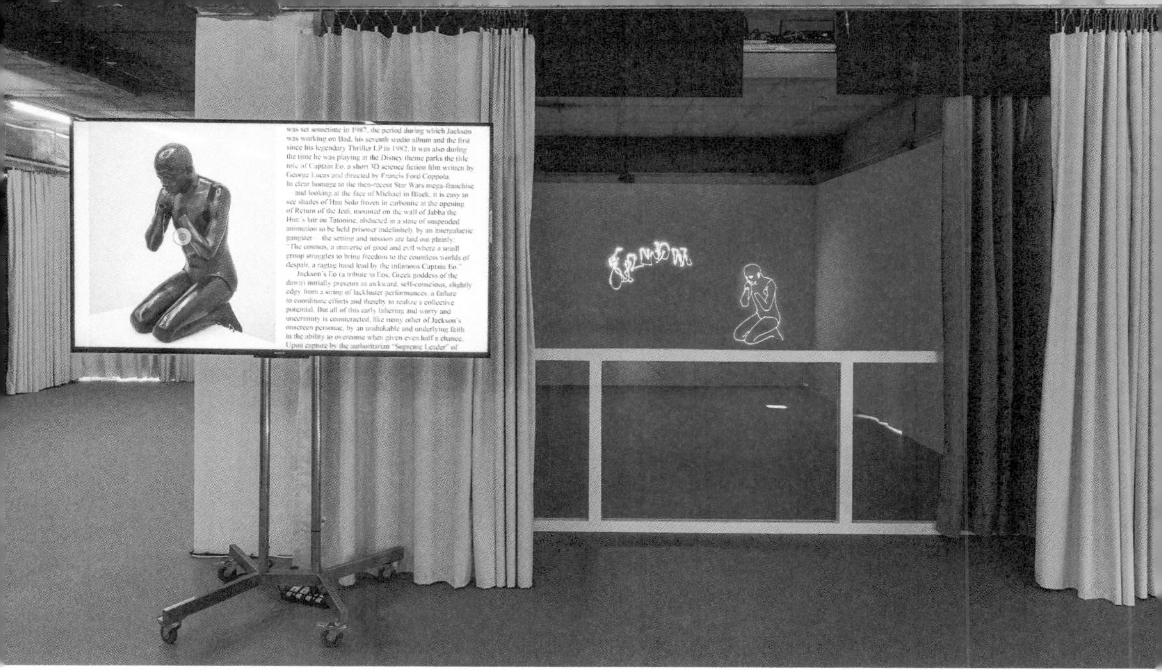

Installation views, Department of Flying Saucers, Fikra Graphic Design Biennial, Sharjah, 2018.

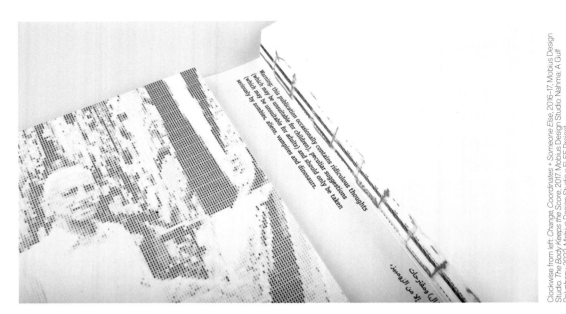

Clockwise from left: *Change, Coordinates + Someone Else*, 2016–17, Mobius Design Studio. *The Body Keeps the Score*, 2017. Mobius Design Studio. Nahma: A Gulf Polyphony, 2022, Mobius Design Studio x FLEE Project.

craftspeople from India; there was this sudden reckoning with India's rich legacy of craft, primarily because the label of Dior was attached to its objects. But we already know that! Dior's arrival in India is irrelevant. So, we're witnessing this from afar, watching BTS videos of the artisans at work, reading articles about the collection's inspiration(s), looking at the event boasting a star-studded guest list, telling ourselves that this doesn't feel right. The discourse around the event wasn't what it needed to be. Again, we ask: who is it that remains conspicuously absent? Why? It should be simple, but it isn't. This disquieting reality hit us in the face because we are all implicated. Just as in Fareej Al Murrar, labour and the source of the artistry are always lost in the allure of the finished product.

We decided to call our project *Crystal No. 6*, a homage to the hands that have to painstakingly place tiny beads in a sequence. From the outset we were very conscious of being outsiders, all women in a male-dominated space, wanting to meet with shop owners and artisans in their private areas and ask them questions. Is our presence problematic? Our hovering? Are we trespassing? Who are we to ask questions anyway? On our first visit, we were relieved to see that our interest was met with excitement, particularly by one shopkeeper's nephew, Aftab, who is very close to our age, and who eagerly introduced us to various people, translating from English to Arabic, to Hindi and to Urdu.

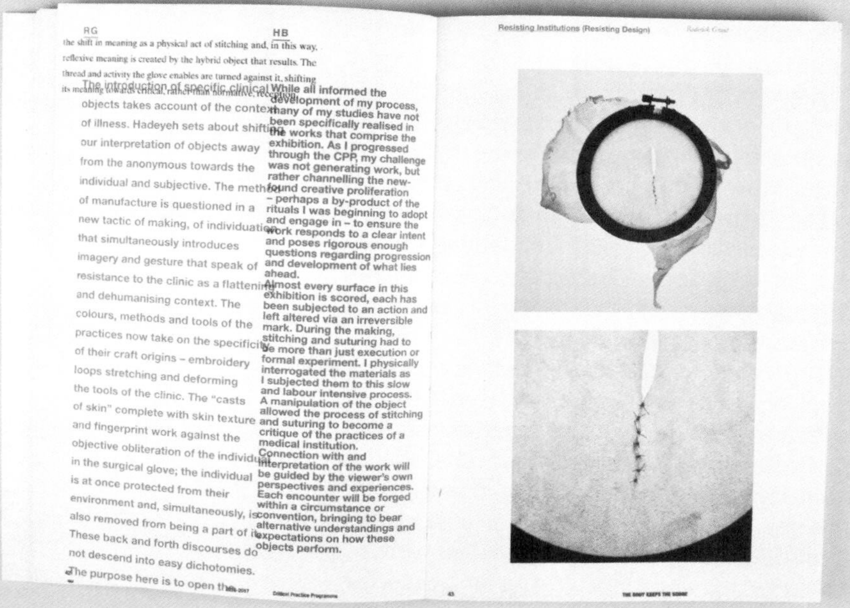

RG HB

Resisting Institutions (Resisting Design) Roderick Grant

the shift in meaning as a physical act of stitching and, in this way, reflexive meaning is created by the hybrid object that results. The thread and activity the glove enables are turned against it, shifting its meaning towards critical, rather than normative, reception.

The introduction of specific clinical objects takes account of the context of illness. Hadeyeh sets about shifting our interpretation of objects away from the anonymous towards the individual and subjective. The method of manufacture is questioned in a new tactic of making, of individuation that simultaneously introduces imagery and gesture that speak of resistance to the clinic as a flattening and dehumanising context. The colours, methods and tools of the practices now take on the specificity of their craft origins – embroidery loops stretching and deforming the tools of the clinic. The "casts of skin" complete with skin texture and fingerprint work against the objective obliteration of the individual in the surgical glove; the individual is at once protected from their environment and, simultaneously, is also removed from being a part of it. These back and forth discourses do not descend into easy dichotomies. The purpose here is to open th

While all informed the development of my process, many of my studies have not been specifically realised in the works that comprise the exhibition. As I progressed through the CPP, my challenge was not generating work, but rather channelling the new-found creative proliferation – perhaps a by-product of the rituals I was beginning to adopt and engage in – to ensure the work responds to a clear intent and poses rigorous enough questions regarding progression and development of what lies ahead.

Almost every surface in this exhibition is scored, each has been subjected to an action and left altered via an irreversible mark. During the making, stitching and suturing had to be more than just execution or formal experiment. I physically interrogated the materials as I subjected them to this slow and labour intensive process. A manipulation of the object allowed the process of stitching and suturing to become a critique of the practices of a medical institution.

Connection with and interpretation of the work will be guided by the viewer's own perspectives and experiences. Each encounter will be forged within a circumstance or convention, bringing to bear alternative understandings and expectations on how these objects perform.

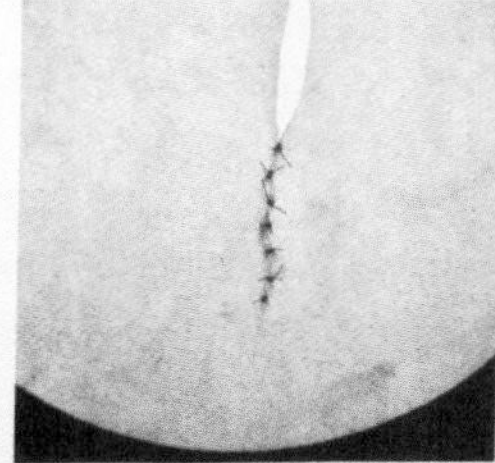

2016-2017 Critical Practice Programme 43 THE BODY KEEPS THE SCORE

Nahma: A Gulf Polyphony

نغمة: بوليفونية خليجية

Nahma: A Gulf Polyphony

For this project, we've made stretchers or *adda*, similar to the wooden frames used by the artisans in the embroidery shops we visited, where we attempted to change the customary dynamics of a commission by asking each artisan what they'd like to embroider, using the technique of their choice. In the exhibition space, we invite visitors to sit on cushions in front of these stretchers, emulating the experience of the seated artisan, in an effort to build empathy and an understanding of how the clothes we wear are made. We share their stories through videos, capturing the usually unseen facets of the process of making, complemented by a publication that offers insight into the history but also the political and social implications of the craft.

Most of the projects we develop or exhibitions we curate are about looking inward and addressing issues that resonate with us personally. Working together over the past 12 years, the three of us have developed telepathic skills. Without saying anything, everybody knows what everybody else is doing. It's partially romantic, partially confusing, partially messy, partially poetic — all words that could be used to describe us. We never labelled or confined ourselves in any way, which is a major reason we started this studio, although there was an external imposition of what this 'discipline' should 'look like'. Now, the reality is different. We wonder how things would have been if we had started three years ago. Our naivety is what propelled us—among other things of course.

We don't really talk about ourselves individually, which is why it's very hard for people to picture us separately, but we're quite animated characters, as you'd expect. Each of us has our own interests, our own vices and virtues, our own demons, our own strengths and struggles. We also celebrate this individuality and push ourselves to explore things independently. Hadeyeh is a textile artist interested in fibre practice, and everything that revolves around making, sourcing, weaving, dyeing, and looking at textiles. Riem is a writer and uses that medium as a means of introspection and linking design theory to creative work. Hala has moved into material exploration and making objects. But that's just a small facet of each person's own 'being human' thing. When one of us is inspired, the other two are fully on board to support that endeavour and it helps our relationship as colleagues, but also as friends.

Mobius Design Studio

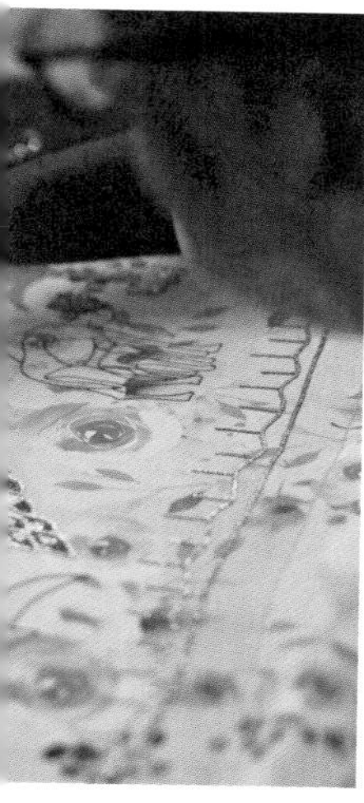

Crystal No. 6, 2024 (detail), 2024, Mobius Design Studio, with process image and sample tracing patterns.

Mobius Design Studio is a UAE-based design studio founded by Hadeyeh Badri, Hala Al-Ani and Riem Ibrahim. Their practice is deeply rooted in education and empowering design practice and research in UAE and the region. *Crystal No. 6* is an installation that presents intricately embroidered self-portraits on wooden stretchers made by artisans in the Freej Al-Murrar neighbourhood in Dubai. With the accompanying texts and videos spotlighting artisans' identities and the stories behind these hand-embroidered garments, the project aims to foster recognition, appreciation and ethical accountability by shifting focus to artisans, while also bridging the gap between art and their highly skilled craft.

Crystal No. 6, 2024, Mobius Design Studio. Exhibition view, *Arab Design Now*, 2024.

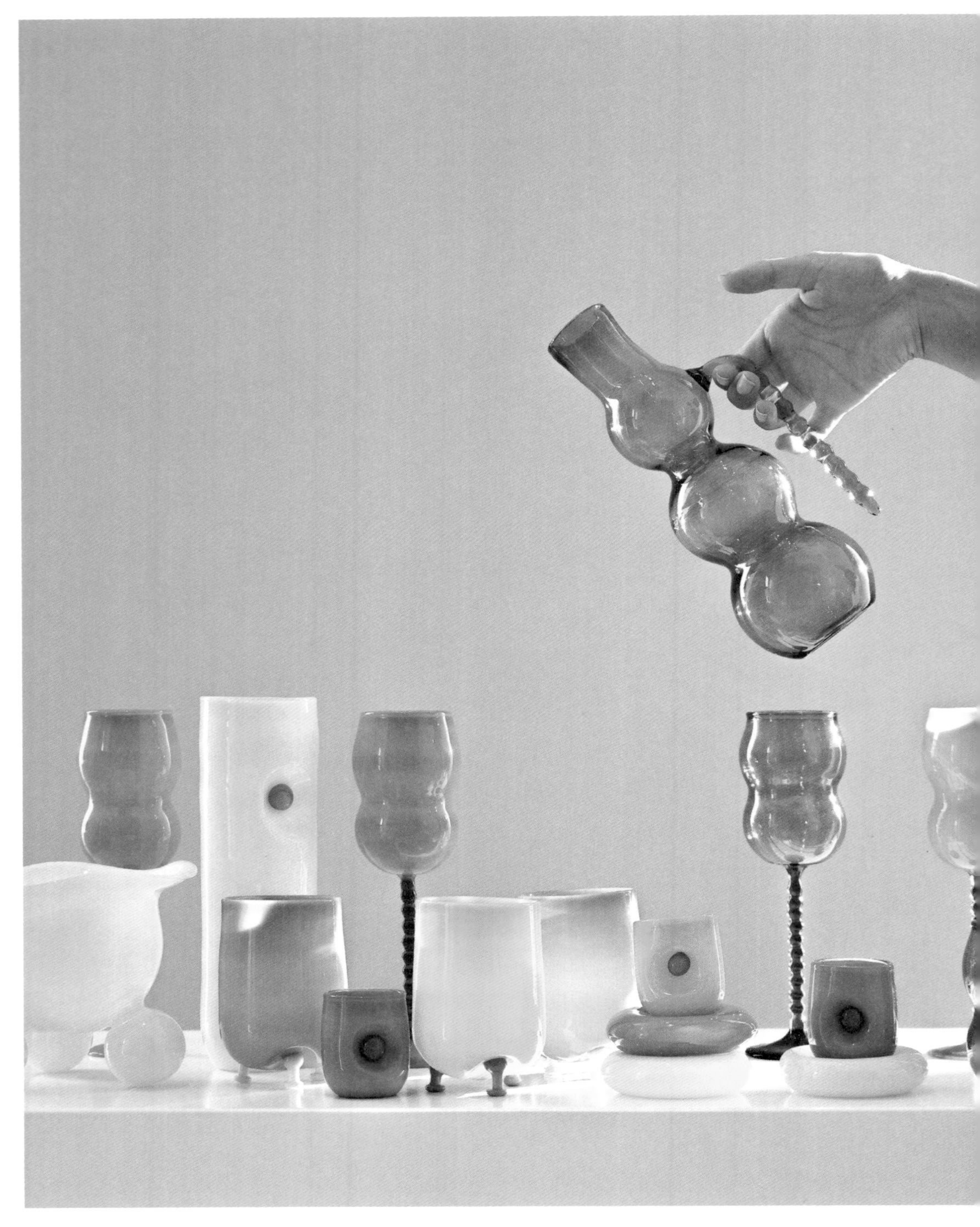

Glass Collection 2020–2022, Ornamental by Lameice.

Lameice Abu Aker, founder of Ornamental by Lameice, is a versatile designer based between Milan and Jerusalem, whose work infuses traditional glassblowing skills with a modern sensibility, while fostering active partnerships with artisans from across Palestine. Her glass pieces were created in the small village of Jaba' in Palestine by the Twam family, known for preserving their artisanal experience over generations. Made from borosilicate glass, the pieces are formed using various processes including blowing, lampworking, and shaping.

Ornamental by Lameice

Dreamlike Glasses, 2022, Ornamental by Lameice.

Bokja is a Beirut-based design studio founded by Maria Hibri and Huda Baroudi. Using embroidery and textiles to create a range of objects, from furniture to wearable fashion, their practice is committed to zero-waste and empowering regional craft communities. *Mashrabiya* is a reinterpretation of the ornate veiled surfaces common in Islamic architecture, and uses Bokja's signature assemblage aesthetic, bringing together textile fragments from a particular time and place, and situating them in unusual arrangements. Composed of modular adjustable units, its malleable nature references a sense of openness, autonomy and transparency, adapting to any context it may occupy.

Mashrabiya, 2015, Bokja.

"To create is to have the urge to tell stories and share narratives through personable objects, from furniture to wearables. Manifesting a zero waste policy and empowerment of regional craft communities are instinctively built in our essence since our inception."

Maria Hibri and Huda Baroudi

Mashrabiya, 2015, Bokja.

Ishraq and Tasneem Zraikat are a design collective based between the US and Jordan working on joint projects that bridge traditional architecture, fibre art, and craft heritage. *Al Matwa* is an homage to the traditional Middle Eastern linen closet typical of regional architecture. The installation recreates this long-lost domestic feature by stacking several wool stuffed mattresses and blankets within a niche. The mattresses and blankets are hand-upholstered in Jordan by expert artisans utilising traditional techniques. The wool used is from the native Jordanian Awassi sheep, and hand-processed by Bedouin women, while the textiles used for the covers of the mattresses and blankets are a mix of new silk, cotton and repurposed vintage fabrics.

Al Matwa, 2024, Ishraq and Tasneem Zraikat. Exhibition view, *Arab Design Now*, 2024.

Ishraq and Tasneem Zraikat

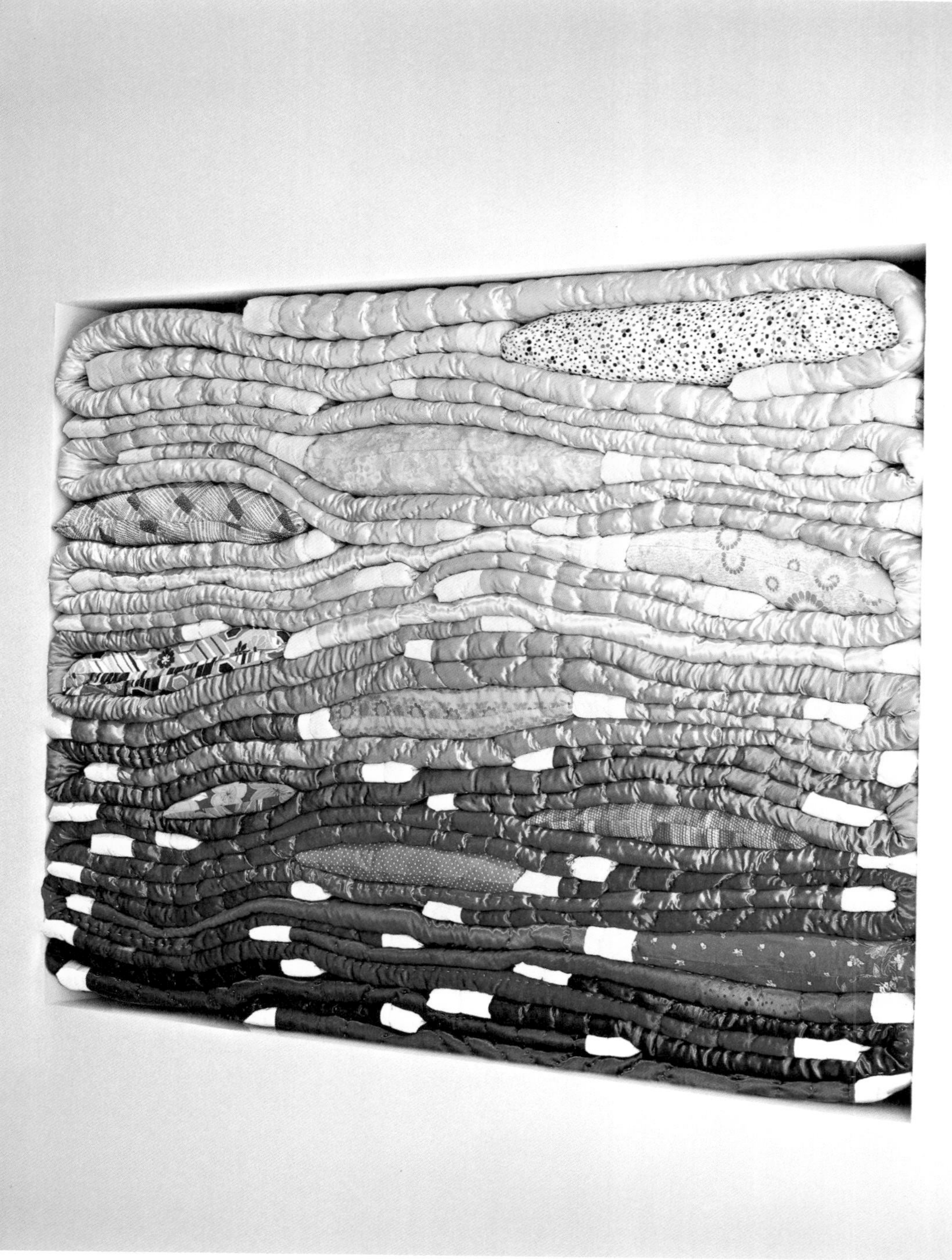

"We tap into our rich culture and craft heritage and discover the innovations of our ancestors who relied on local resources for most of their needs. It is about discovering our past technologies and their products, which have withstood the test of time."

Ishraq and Tasneem Zraikat

Al Matwa, 2024, (detail) Ishraq and Tasneem Zraikat.

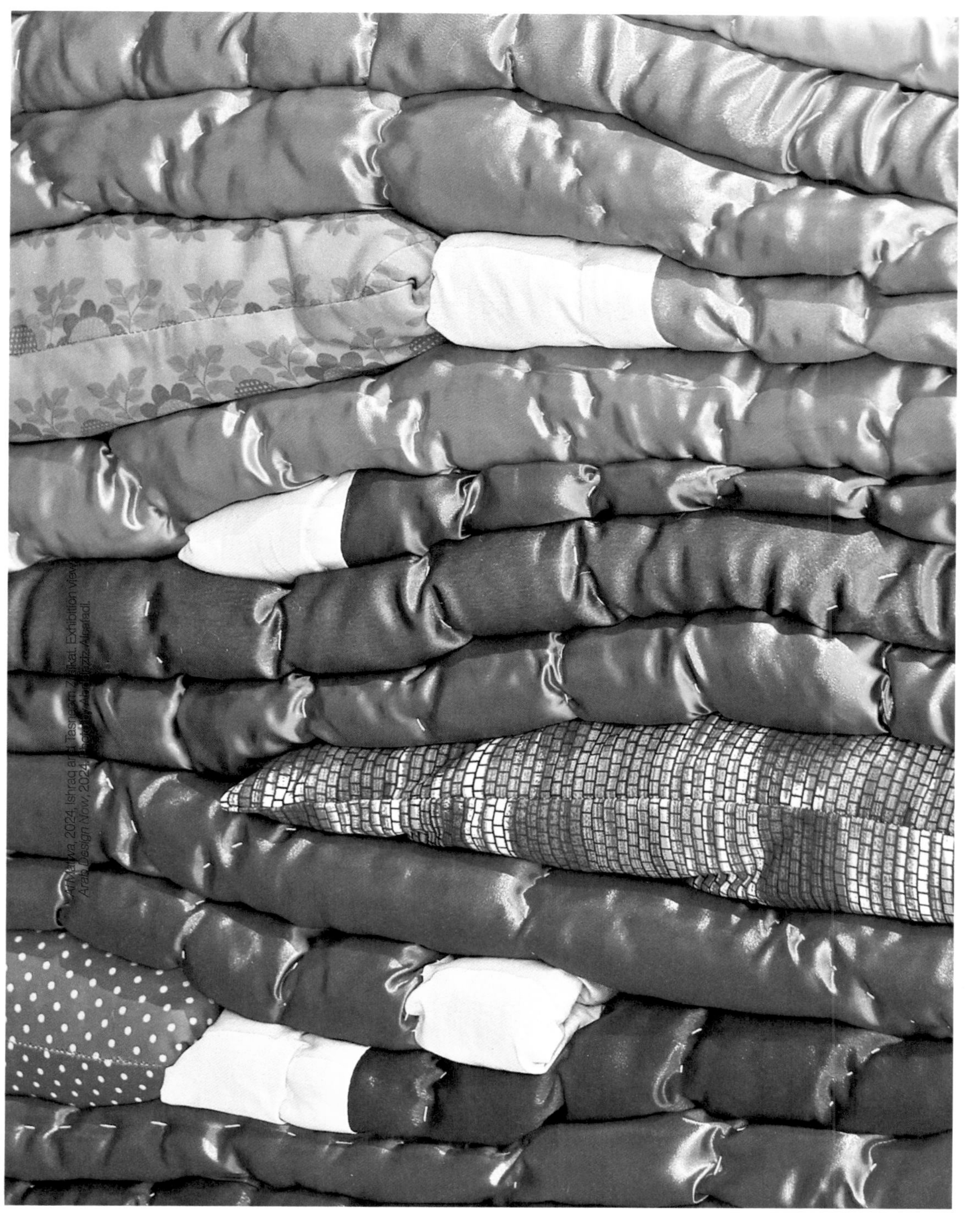

Al Matwa, 2024, Ishraq and Tasneem Zraikat. Exhibition view Arab Design Now, 2024, photo by Abdelaziz Alsefadi.